BETTY
FORD

MODERN FIRST LADIES

Lewis L. Gould, Editor

TITLES IN THE SERIES

Jacqueline Kennedy: First Lady of the New Frontier, Barbara A. Perry

Lady Bird Johnson: Our Environmental First Lady, Lewis L. Gould

BETTY FORD

CANDOR AND COURAGE IN

THE WHITE HOUSE

JOHN ROBERT GREENE

UNIVERSITY PRESS OF KANSAS

BIO
FORD
BETTY

© 2004 by the University Press of Kansas
All rights reserved
Published by the University Press of Kansas
(Lawrence, Kansas 66049), which was organized by
the Kansas Board of Regents and is operated and
funded by Emporia State University, Fort Hays State
University, Kansas State University, Pittsburg State
University, the University of Kansas, and Wichita
State University
Library of Congress Cataloging-in-Publication Data
Greene, John Robert, 1955–
Betty Ford : candor and courage in the White
House / John Robert Greene.
p.   cm. — (Modern first ladies)
Includes bibliographical references and index.
ISBN 0-7006-1354-4 (cloth : alk. paper)
1. Ford, Betty, 1918– 2. Presidents' spouses—
United States—Biography. I. Title. II. Series.
E867.F67G74 2004
973.925'092—dc22   2004013586

British Library Cataloguing-in-Publication Data
is available.
Printed in the United States of America
10 9 8 7 6 5 4 3 2 1
The paper used in this publication meets the
minimum requirements of the American National
Standard for Permanence of Paper for Printed
Library Materials Z39.48-1984.

For Patty, T. J., Christopher, and Mary Rose

Books are the children of the brain.

—Jonathan Swift

and Jenny Madeleine Elisabeth Reimann (1953–2004)

Candor and Courage in our Family

Come trip it lightly, as you go on the light fantastic toe.
—Quote accompanying the senior class photo of Betty Bloomer,
Central High (Grand Rapids) Yearbook, 1936.

Somehow we [women] always feel we *must* be there . . . And all the
while *paining*. Women call it 'being a woman.' And by golly,
I'm sure that describes the noble woman, Betty Ford.
—Pearl Bailey

CONTENTS

Editor's Foreword

xi

Preface

xiii

CHAPTER 1: Dancer

1

CHAPTER 2: "The Congress Got a Minority Leader, and I Lost a Husband"

16

CHAPTER 3: "She Was Beginning to Flower a Little"

38

CHAPTER 4: "I Just Figured that It Was Time that Somebody Spoke Up"

66

CHAPTER 5: The "First Mama" and the Election of 1976

83

CHAPTER 6: "My Name Is Betty Ford . . ."

101

CHAPTER 7: Legacy

117

Notes

125

Bibliographic Essay

145

Index

157

EDITOR'S FOREWORD

During her husband's brief presidency, Betty Ford became celebrated for her outspoken views on abortion and the Equal Rights Amendment, her courage when facing breast cancer, and her sense of fun in the White House. Revelations about her battle with prescription drugs and alcohol, culminating in a family intervention and eventually the creation of the Betty Ford Center, made her even more of a national figure after her husband's presidency ended. She exemplified determination in the face of human trials and an irrepressible sense of courage in her public appearances. Her fame did not recede in the years when she was no longer first lady. If anything, her status as a role model for people with addictions and personal pain became more pronounced.

The roots of Betty Ford's problems and triumphs lay in her childhood in Grand Rapids, Michigan. In the first study to trace the origins of her demons and the ways she battled them during her husband's career, John Robert Greene has combined fresh research with his wide knowledge of the Ford era to produce a book that illuminates how Betty Ford became the woman that Americans have admired. Greene shows that alcoholism in Betty Ford's family was a pervasive problem, and he examines how she interacted with her addiction when her husband was in the House of Representatives, vice president, and then president from 1974 to 1977. Despite these unresolved emotional and medical issues, in the White House, Mrs. Ford managed to be a free spirit. Greene surveys her struggle with breast cancer, her advocacy of the Equal Rights Amendment, and her role in the 1976 election campaign with skill and insight. His capacity to maintain his balance in discussing both the positive and negative aspects of Betty Ford's performance in the White House makes this volume a notable contribution to the Modern First Ladies series. It also shows why a generation of Americans found in Betty Ford such an attractive and human woman during a difficult time for the nation. The pressures of being the first lady in the unrelenting media spotlight almost consumed Betty Ford, but she maintained her indomitable sense of self. In the end, she overcame her challenges and found a healthy place in society. In this engaging and fascinating book, John Robert Greene shows why her story says so much about an independent first lady and her lasting impact on an important American institution.

PREFACE

In all polls, whether conducted by an academic or for the general public, Betty Bloomer Warren Ford is consistently rated as one of the top ten most successful and respected first ladies in American history. She is universally lauded for her courage and candor, as observers point to her fights against three diseases—substance abuse, arthritis, and breast cancer. She is remembered in popular literature and popular magazine retrospectives for her public battles against these demons. Indeed, in a poll conducted by the television network VH1 in 2003 to identify "The 200 Greatest Pop Culture Icons," Betty came in 166th—only one place better than the Three Stooges.[1]

Clearly, Americans have reacted to Betty Ford, rather than evaluated her. She is included in the usual encyclopedias and readers on the first ladies, and along with the story of her lifelong battle for her health, she is given credit for taking a public stand in favor of the Equal Rights Amendment, speaking candidly regarding her relationship with her children on *60 Minutes,* and for being the most outspoken first lady since Eleanor Roosevelt. Some observers go so far as to call her an "active political partner of the president" and suggest that she had a role in driving the policy agenda of the Ford White House. However, there has been little analysis beyond these claims. No scholarly biography of Betty Ford has been published that makes use of the vast amount of available archival and manuscript material; nor has a detailed study of her important and influential tenure as first lady been offered. The success or failure of her advocacy, as well as the impact of her twenty-nine-month tenure as first lady, have not been fully evaluated.

1. For more information, see the VH1 Web site, at http://www.vh1.com/shows/dyn/the_greatest/68030/episode_wildcard.jhtml?wildcard=/shows/dynamic/includes/wildcards/the_greatest/200_greatest_icons/ranked_list/161_180_aux.jhtml&event_id=865273.

Until recently, the same was true of her husband. Choosing to like the affable Gerald Ford rather than think about him, scholars had essentially taken a pass on a detailed analysis of his presidency. In 1995 I fired the opening salvo in a scholarly analysis of Gerald Ford[2]; it is, perhaps, fitting that I now take a shot at a scholarly analysis of Betty Ford. In so doing, one of the limitations of my book on Gerald Ford has became embarrassingly evident. As I began to detail for myself the impact of Betty Ford as first lady, I realized not just how much of an impact she had on the Ford Administration—indeed, I concluded that she succeeded in areas where her husband had tried and failed, and she developed into much more than had been expected of a traditional first lady—but that I had seriously downplayed that impact in my work on the Ford Administration. Although I like to think that this revelation shows some growth on my part as a historian, the reality is that historians have yet to adequately analyze and discuss the role of the first lady in American political history. I am certain that the series of which this book is a part will go a long way toward addressing that gap; I hope that this book will be a step toward addressing this in terms of Betty Ford.

Writers only *write* alone. (Indeed, if they have small children, writing alone is a luxury that occurs all too infrequently—with this in mind, thanks once again to the Clark family.) Indeed, one of the greatest pleasures of any writing project is to freely admit that there is a list of names without any of whom this book could not have been written. Although Betty Ford declined to be interviewed for this book, I am grateful to James Cannon, Maria Downs, and Jack Ford for taking the time to talk to me about Betty Ford. Thanks to Maria Downs for permission to use her unpublished memoir, *Mostly Wine and Roses,* and to Tina Mion for permission to use her extraordinary portrait of Mrs. Ford, found in Chapter 6. No work on the Ford Administration can be undertaken without utilizing the collections housed at the Gerald R. Ford Library. For my money, the staff at the Ford Library is the best in the business; I thank the director, Dennis Dallenbach; and David Horrocks,

2. John Robert Greene, *The Presidency of Gerald R. Ford* (Lawrence: University Press of Kansas, 1995).

Helmi Raaska, and William McNitt for their service to this writer. Nancy Mirshah of the GFL went far beyond the call of duty in helping me track down the photos that add to this book. Likewise, I thank the staff of my home library at Cazenovia College, and I apologize to director Stanley Kozaczka and to Judy Azzoto and Nan Bailey for my countless bibliographic requests. I have also had the aid of several outstanding student research assistants: Lindsay Bednarczyk, Amber Farr, Mara Hogan, Marcie Palmer, and Melissa Zomro. Connie Hildreth helped organize my professional life—a herculean task if ever there was one.

Several colleagues read the manuscript with a critical eye, pointed out errors of thought and detail, and helped shape the final effort into a more solid argument. I thank Susan Goodier and Grazyna Kozaczka of Cazenovia College for reading the entire book manuscript while it was in its infancy. Susan M. Hartmann of Ohio State University offered a thorough analysis of the initial draft that was indispensable in aiding me with my revisions. Finally, Lewis Gould of the University of Texas, the series editor for the Modern First Ladies series, has read every word, and he has not only been a balanced critic of my work, but also a tireless advocate for the project. Last, I am grateful to those at the University Press of Kansas who have worked with me over the years and have turned my writing into books of which I am proud: production editor Larisa Martin, copy editor Karen Hellekson, and assistant director and marketing manager Susan Schott. I am particularly in debt to director Fred Woodward for his imagination and support of my writing ventures. I am pleased to call the University Press of Kansas my literary home.

Betty Ford, official first lady portrait (1974)
(courtesy of the Gerald R. Ford Library).

BETTY
FORD

CHAPTER 1

DANCER

Elizabeth Ann Bloomer was born on April 8, 1918, in Chicago's Lake View Hospital. Betty (who remembered that "I always wanted to be called Elizabeth, but it never happened") was the youngest of three children; a brother, William Jr., was seven years her senior, and another brother, Robert, was five years older. Betty seems to have been an unexpected addition to the Bloomer household. Her mother, Hortense Neahr Bloomer, was thirty-five, then of an age when childbearing caused great concern—she would later revel in retelling the quip that Betty had popped out of a bottle of champagne.[1]

Betty's first home was an apartment building in East Rogers Park, a fast-growing, affluent suburb of Chicago. Shortly after her birth, the family moved to Denver; then, in 1920, they settled in Grand Rapids, Michigan. Nestled on the banks of western Michigan's Grand River, the city was the epitome of Middle America in the 1920s. Populated largely by the descendants of Dutch emigrants who came to the area immediately after the Civil War, the town was known for the furniture its several factories turned out. The Christian Reformed Church and the Reformed Church of America, two rather austere Calvinist denominations, set the tone for the mores and values of the community. Its public schools were consistently rated among the best in the country, it was second in the nation in home ownership, and it was first in the country in tree ownership per citizen. All in all, Grand Rapids was a perfect place to raise a family.[2]

On its surface, Betty's early life fit neatly into this idyllic midwestern stereotype. Her father, a traveling salesperson for the Royal Rubber Company who sold conveyor belts to factories, prospered throughout the 1920s, thanks to the rise of the automobile. The combination of Bloomer's business success and Hortense's social contacts (she came from a wealthy family, and among her causes was her presidency of the crippled children's home in Grand Rapids) led to a comfortable existence for the Bloomers. They lived in a home in a fashionable section of Grand Rapids, and in her memoirs, Betty wistfully recalled the summers at the family cottage on Michigan's Whitefish Lake, a high-status retreat for the moderately wealthy. The Bloomers were even well insulated from the most calamitous event in American history. The stock market crash of 1929, which occurred when Betty was eleven years old, largely passed the family by—Betty would remember that during the first years of the Great Depression, her family only had to "cut back."[3]

Hortense also saw to it that, like she had been, her daughter was exposed to the best that Grand Rapids society had to offer. As a teen, Betty was a member of a service sorority (Gamma Delta Tau), as well as the Junior League of Grand Rapids, where she was an active participant in many of its projects. Her participation in these organizations earned for Betty her first press coverage in 1934 and 1936: the *Grand Rapids Press* ran her photograph on the front page of its society section.[4]

Thanks largely to the influence of her strong-willed mother, Betty was no shrinking violet. The Bloomer family pitted two older brothers against one little sister. Betty could have withdrawn from her boisterous siblings and become a bookish recluse, so as to save herself from the teasing and the brawling. But this did not happen. She developed into a rowdy shadow to her brothers; when she told a biographer in 1974, "I guess I was a tomboy," she sorely understated the case. Betty prided herself on her willingness to jump into a pile of prepubescent males and join in their fights. She also joined them in their football and ice hockey games—when allowed by her brothers. Indeed, she had to be told by her mother to stop running around the upstairs of their home without any clothes on; to Betty, a girl who felt that she was just one of the boys, such restrictions "didn't make sense to me"[5] (Figure 1.1).

Yet beneath this apparently pleasant surface were truths that boded ill for Betty's future. For the entirety of her young life, she was, for all intents and purposes, denied the steadying influence of a father. Despite the financial security that he provided his family, even through tough times, Bill Bloomer was chiefly distinguished in the life of his children by his absence. Indeed, largely because business was so good, he was on the road a great deal. Betty would later say, "I regretted the fact that I didn't get to know him." This feeling of loss would soon be compounded by Bloomer's death in 1934, when Betty was sixteen. The story in the Grand Rapids newspapers was that he asphyxiated in his garage while underneath the family car, trying to make repairs. There was, however, some speculation at the time that he had committed suicide. But the report of the coroner's, as recorded on Bloomer's death certificate, would seem to put the matter to rest: the "principal cause of death" was "carbon monoxide poisoning," and the death was officially ruled "accidental."[6]

Yet Bloomer's death would not ultimately be as important to his daughter as a fact regarding his life that she learned from her mother at his funeral. Bill Bloomer suffered from alcoholism. Hortense had, in effect, been her husband's enabler by keeping the truth about his disease from her children (Betty would later remember that "occasionally, Mother would say to me, 'Your dad's not feeling well. I'm going to go out there [on the road] and see him because I'm lonely.' I think she had to go rescue him.") Two of his children—his son Bob and his daughter Betty—would share his disease. Since the 1970s, much research has been done on the question of whether or not alcoholism is hereditary. Scientists have yet to isolate a genetic component that will establish once and for all the hereditary nature of the disease. Nevertheless, it has clearly been established by these studies that alcoholism is a family disease. Although the profile does not, in some ways, fit Betty (according to studies, for example, most alcoholic women "had no particularly strong ties to either parent or to any of their siblings"), she otherwise fits the profile of the female alcoholic child of an alcoholic parent quite neatly. Studies note that

Figure 1.1. Betty Bloomer, age fourteen (1932)
(courtesy of the Gerald R. Ford Library).

in about 42 percent of the cases, the father of a female alcoholic is an absent parent. Approximately the same percentage of patients reported problem drinking by one or more of their parents. None of these patients had parents who were in a happy marriage, and a high percentage of them reported that they had a strict, controlling, perfectionist mother.[7]

Thanks to Bloomer's absences and alcoholism, Hortense was the leading influence in Betty's early life. Intensely formal, domineering by nature (a friend of Betty's remembered later that Hortense "commanded respect"; if you stood next to her, "you stood a little straighter"), and forced by circumstances to assume the dual roles of father and mother even before her husband's death, Hortense kept a tight rein on her household. Her discipline was hardly subtle. It ranged from demanding that her daughter wear formal white gloves when shopping, to her strategy for dealing with Betty's prepubescent proclivity for snacking in between meals—she hung a sign on her daughter's back that said, "Please Do Not Feed This Child." Hortense was also her daughter's most severe critic. Betty would later remember: "Once, when I was dancing in the high-school follies, I did sort of a sloppy job, and she saw the performance. When I got home that night, she told me straight: 'If you don't do it well, don't do it at all.' She expected perfection." This is not to say that Hortense was not capable of compassion and encouragement. But even her caring seemed designed to strengthen her daughter for the challenges to come. For example, one day Betty was teased in school for having a birthmark on her left arm, and as a result, she came home crying. Her mother simply told her that the birthmark made her a "very special child."[8]

It took time for Betty to come to grips with the true impact of Hortense on her personality and upbringing. In a 1976 interview specifically dealing with the relationship between her and her mother, Betty claimed that "the greatest desire of my life was to be half as perfect as my mother was." However, only three years later— but after she had gone through rigorous treatment for substance abuse—Betty felt differently: "It was a burden to live up to her expectations; she was a perfectionist, which, I am sure, is why I am. I'm trying very hard not to put that burden on [Betty's daughter] Susie. . . . I am sure my mother was a frustrated woman. There were so many things missing in her life."[9]

As a child of the 1920s and 1930s, and one who was largely reared by a mother of strength and fortitude, Betty Bloomer developed into the epitome of what many observers have casually labeled the first "modern woman." This was a time of immense change for young women, who in the era between the wars were pursuing an independence of spirit heretofore unheard of in American history. From new, revealing modes of dress, to sexually charged dances like the Charleston, to demanding tobacco and alcohol (regardless of Prohibition) in public, young women were demonstrating their desire to escape from a rather austere Victorianism and to enjoy life. These changes did not pass by America's heartland. Indeed, Betty Bloomer and her friends, members of a high school sorority nicknamed the "Good Cheers," rather typified the new spirit of young women in the 1920s. They went to parties together and even chased boys for sport. (Betty was a notorious flirt, chasing after a boy who was believed to be unattainable, convincing him to give her his fraternity pin, then coquettishly returning the pin and moving on to the next conquest.) Most of the Good Cheers smoked; Betty had her first cigarette at age fourteen. Her parents had promised each of their children five hundred dollars if they didn't smoke before they reached the age of twenty-one; Betty remembered that "my brother Bill was the only one who collected." Betty even remembered taking her first drink at this early age.[10]

Thus, Betty Bloomer developed into a much more independent woman than even her mother. And this was not solely a case of youthful passion run amok. She had a serious independence of mind that set her apart from her peers. This was foreshadowed in a decision of some import, made before her father's death. Betty decided to adopt her mother's religion over her father's, and was christened in the Episcopal Church when she was fourteen. Despite her strength of character, such behavior was alien to Hortense, but none was more so than her daughter's stubborn desire to become a dancer.[11]

No less an impresario than Martha Graham, who would mentor Betty Bloomer, summarized the calling felt by the performing artist in her memoir, *Blood Memory*: "People have asked me why I chose to be a dancer. I did not choose. I was chosen to be a dancer, and with that, you live all your life." And yet as with most things, the spark for one of the most important decisions in Betty's life came from her mother. Although Betty originally wanted to learn to play piano, Hortense enrolled her daughter in dance lessons. No reason for this decision has survived, but dancing quickly progressed from a childhood obligation (Betty later observed that her mother might have enrolled her to overcome her clumsiness) to a lifelong love affair with the art (Figure 1.2). Quite simply, to Betty, "dance was my happiness." She began her lessons at age eight, studying with Calla Travis of Grand Rapids. Betty helped pay for the expensive lessons by working as a fashion model at Herpolscheimer's department store, where she walked through the crowds telling potential customers about the assets of the new misses outfits she was wearing—thus beginning a relationship with the fashionable department store that would last, with but a few interruptions, until she left for Washington in 1948. For four summers, beginning in 1937, she was also a dance instructor at Camp Bryn Afom, a private camp for affluent girls on Michigan's Stone Lake. Betty made a splash by dancing in leotards, hardly an accepted mode of dress for a young lady in the 1930s. She graduated from Travis's academy in 1935, then began giving lessons herself. She opened the Betty Bloomer School of Dance in a friend's basement, charging half the tuition that Travis charged and operating one day a week. She had found her calling. Modeling, dancing, teaching—Betty Bloomer loved being on stage.[12]

Betty briefly thought of becoming a ballerina, but she had to admit, "I was probably the worst ballet dancer who ever came down the road. I couldn't get my knees straight enough." Instead, she gravitated toward modern dance. Free-flowing, athletic, and extemporaneous, modern dance used the dancer's body as the conveyor of the message. One useful definition of the art is that it "simply rediscovers what the body can do." Graham chose to define the medium by using a term that would title one of her most famous compositions, one that illustrated the discipline that she felt modern dancers must attain: "dancers are the Acrobats of God." The freedom that modern dance exhibited paralleled the freedom of the spirit felt by younger women in the interwar years. For the outgoing Betty, one hardly prone to automatically accept convention as an artistic constant, it was a perfect match.[13]

Immediately upon her 1936 graduation from Central High School, Betty made it clear to her mother that she wanted dance as a career, and that, as she later remembered, "there was no sense wasting time in an academic college." She began to pester Hortense to let her move to New York City to study dance. To this point, Hortense had seen dance simply as a hobby for her daughter, who she seemed

Figure 1.2. Betty Bloomer dancing (1934)
(courtesy of the Gerald R. Ford Library).

to assume would follow in her footsteps as a society matron. Hortense was as adamant in her disapproval as her daughter was persistent. Thus, a deal was struck. Over two summers, Hortense temporarily deferred the New York question by allowing Betty to attend the Bennington School of Dance, a highly regarded school that was affiliated with Bennington College in Vermont.[14]

An institution with an international reputation for its progressive atmosphere toward intellectual pursuits, Bennington could boast of having philosopher Joseph Campbell, psychologist Eric Fromm, and the poets Ben Belitt and William Carlos Williams on its faculty. In dance, the faculty was among the best in the world, including Anna Sokolov, Charles Weidman, and Doris Humphrey. But one instructor completely changed Betty's life. Next to her future husband and president of the United States, no person had more of an influence on Betty than did Martha Graham. Graham, born in Pittsburgh in 1894 and raised in Santa Barbara, California, began her career in 1916, dancing with the Denishawn Company (founded by modern dance pioneers Ruth St. Denis and Ted Shawn) of Los Angeles. Sparked by Graham's talent, Shawn began to choreograph solos just for her. These solos led to Graham's being asked to perform as a soloist in the popular Greenwich Village Follies, giving her her first taste of New York. In 1925, Graham temporarily abandoned her New York career and accepted a teaching position at the Eastman School of Dance in Rochester, New York. However, her tenure lasted only one year. As she later remembered, "what the people in Rochester did not understand was that dance was going to develop into an art, and not remain an entertainment in the spirit of Radio City Music Hall." She quit and started her own dance company, opening a studio back in Greenwich Village.[15]

Graham's compositions and performances changed the face of the dance world. As important as the radically new technique of modern dance was the fact that in the middle of the Depression, Graham's compositions included social content that was far from mainstream. Her 1930 ballet, "Lamentation," for example, was a solo dance where she wore a long tube of material designed to show the tragedy within the human body. Her teaching was no less important or revolutionary. When she severed herself from Denishawn, Shawn and St. Denis required that Graham, like all their former students, pay a fee if she wished to teach Denishawn methods. As one scholar of Graham's work has noted, "this proved to be a blessing in disguise, because it forced Graham to evolve her own teaching methods." Her signature style of teaching her students to express primal emotions through their body movements was so innovative that it was eventually copyrighted as the Graham Technique. She honed her technique at Eastman and perfected it at both her New York studio and at Bennington College. Graham began spending her summers in Bennington, largely because it was "a wonderful place where we were given the freedom and possibility to make our dances." The effect that she had on her students in every setting was electric.[16]

Betty reveled in her new freedom and in the beauty of summers in Vermont. In 1976, she returned to Bennington to dedicate the college's new Visual and Performing Arts Center; in her remarks, she remembered "being barefoot most of the time and wearing a leotard from dawn to dusk. Between classes we bounced around the green and tried to pick up as much grass as possible with our toes." By her second summer, there was less grass-picking and more serious study, as Betty began to work closely with Graham. Already a free spirit, Betty was entranced with the freedom of Graham's choreography. Betty also had the ability to master the difficult physical regimen necessary for modern dance. The master's rigor was severe, but Betty later remembered it as "exhilarating" (in 1974, in an answer to a question regarding Graham's discipline, Betty remembered that Graham never slapped her "in the face, but I got many a knee in the back"). Perhaps Betty found herself gravitating to a woman who exhibited as strong a personality as her mother ("I admired that kind of strictness"). Regardless, her view of Graham was uncompromising: "I worshipped her as a goddess."[17]

At the end of Betty's second summer at Bennington in 1938, Graham's traveling troupe came to Ann Arbor. After the performance, which Betty attended, she asked her mentor if she could study with her at her Fifth Avenue studio in New York and become a member of the Martha Graham Dance Company—then the oldest modern dance company in America, and today the oldest modern dance company in the world. Graham agreed, and Hortense acquiesced. Betty immediately moved to New York and took an apartment with several other Graham students. She also traded on her training at Herpolscheimer's and got a job with the prestigious John Robert Powers Modeling Agency, where she appeared in many fashion shows. Betty would spend the next three years studying with Graham, but she never made it to the first team. Due, by her own admission, to a rather active social life that "got in the way of my dancing," Betty was not chosen for Graham's road troupe. Rather, she, along with eleven other students, danced with the Assistant Dance Group, which appeared with the main Martha Graham Company when it performed in New York. Playbills exist for two 1938 performances that included Betty, one at Carnegie Hall and one at the Alvin Theatre. The work she danced in was called "American Document," and she may have performed in another Graham work entitled "Primitive Mysteries."[18]

Betty's not being chosen for the travel company gave Hortense the moment she had waited for. In 1941, she proposed a deal to her daughter. Betty would return home to Grand Rapids for six months. If, at the end of that trial period, she wished to return to New York, her mother would not interfere. Betty spoke to Graham, who, perhaps seeing in Betty a woman of talent but without the personal drive to succeed in the business, encouraged her to return to Grand Rapids for the trial period. Betty gave in. Hortense went to New York, collected her daughter, and drove her home.[19]

Upon her return to Grand Rapids, Betty returned to Herpolscheimer's as the store's fashion director. But she by no means gave up her desire to pursue dance, and Calla Travis immediately hired her former student as a teacher. In a later interview, Betty would correctly point out that being a teacher and a fashion director were both acceptable "women's careers" in the late 1930s. But Betty, always precocious and now having been exposed to the bohemian lifestyle of New York, quickly pushed the envelope of artistic tolerance for conservative Grand Rapids. She was publicly criticized for producing a modern dance with scantily clad dancers called "The Three Parables" in a Baptist church. She was more privately criticized for teaching black students.[20]

Regardless of the criticism, Betty had now established herself as a career woman. She traveled widely for Herpolscheimer's, and she had a job on the side to boot. She also had an active social life. She was a regular at parties, and she dated often. Her brother remembered with a smile that "she attracted men . . . I think she liked them all." However, such revelry was challenged by the good old-fashioned middle-class desire to settle down and raise a family. Indeed, her mother had found such stability—a stability she had never

known with Bill Bloomer—in her second husband, Arthur Meigs
Godwin, a Chicago banker whom she had married in 1940. The
Bloomer family had known Godwin for years and had grieved with
him when his first wife was killed in an automobile accident. Now,
Betty asked his permission to call her stepfather "Dad," a permission he readily gave. Hortense was so enraptured with her new love
that she went with him on a world tour for their honeymoon and
ordered Betty to sell her house and all its contents, so that upon
their return, she could quickly move in with her new husband.
However, Godwin had gained more for himself than just a new
wife; soon after their honeymoon, his new stepdaughter also moved
into his house.[21]

Drawn by convention to settle down, yet hardly ready to do so,
Betty tried to find a man who was as much a partier as herself. Her
first attempt came up short. Betty was first engaged to a young lawyer, reported by one biographer to have been from Petoskey, Michigan. In her memoirs, Betty says little of this suitor, except that he
was a "very sober fellow." It does not seem to have been an extraordinarily serious relationship—at least to Betty. Indeed, one biographer asserts that she ended the relationship because of an argument
sparked by Betty spending an evening with her friends that lasted
until she came home at 4:00 AM.[22]

Betty then turned to an old flame who promised her both stability and carousing. Betty had met William Warren at age twelve—he
had taken her to her first dance. He had grown to a handsome and
charming young businessman. He also enjoyed a good party as
much as Betty did, and Warren was enough of a partier to concern
both her mother and stepfather, both of whom made their disapproval of the match well known. Yet Warren had much to offer.
Quite aside from his affable personality, he offered a kind of security
in turbulent times—despite the fact that their friends were leaving
in droves for service in World War II, Warren had diabetes, and thus
he was ineligible for the draft. Betty was smitten, and she soon
began to see Warren exclusively. The couple resorted to lying to
Betty's family about their dates. (Betty told her parents that she was
dating John Locke, and apparently they bought it.) But the charade
was short-lived; Betty confronted her mother with her love for Warren, and her parents acquiesced. The 24-year-old Betty Bloomer

married Warren in her stepfather's living room, on a date that she professes not to remember, but that her divorce decree lists as April 23, 1942.[23]

In the first volume of her memoirs, Betty labels her first marriage as "The Five Year Misunderstanding." Perhaps. And yet Betty should have known what she was getting into. A childhood friend of Betty's remembers Warren as "ambitious . . . which was not right for a young gal who wanted a family and a staid, dependable husband." A salesman like her father, Warren lacked the solidity that her stepfather now offered her mother. Betty later admitted, "we moved around from pillar to post. That was the story of the marriage." It was also an understatement. In a two-year period, the couple lived not only in Grand Rapids, but in towns in Ohio (where Betty continued her trade as a model in a department store outside Toledo, and once took the family shotgun, stuck it out a window, and shot a rabbit for dinner), New York (where Betty took a part-time job in a frozen food factory), and then back to Grand Rapids. There, he took a job as traveling furniture salesman and, like Bill Bloomer, took to the road.[24]

Quite aside from her husband's absences, Betty might have done well to consider an incident in their past, when Warren left her at a high school dance to sneak a beer with his buddies. (Betty slapped him in the face, and exclaimed, "You're not a gentleman. Don't ever bother to call me again.") Indeed, Warren was an alcoholic, and it clearly had an effect on Betty. Already at a higher risk of alcohol abuse because of her father's addiction, she remembered that with her husband gone, "I might just as well head straight for the bar." Although, as noted above, a cause-and-effect relationship has yet to be completely proven, these same studies make one fact plain: "few alcoholic women have happy marriages before their recourse to heavy drinking."[25]

Betty's marriage to Bill Warren profoundly changed her. The professional dancer and self-professed good-time girl was, in her words, "ready for a house and children." The problem was, her husband wasn't. Betty took her job back at Herpolscheimer's, where she was promoted to fashion coordinator. She professes to have tried to keep Warren at home, but to no avail. Betty decided to make a break. She was in the process of writing Warren a letter, telling him not to return to their apartment and that his possessions had been sent to his parents' house, when his office called to tell her that while in Boston, Warren had slipped into a diabetic coma. Temporarily abandoning her plan to leave her husband, Betty rushed to his side. Warren would live, but part of his face had been paralyzed. Betty stayed in Boston for six weeks with friends while her husband's condition stabilized. Warren's parents moved their son onto the porch of their home; his wife slept upstairs. Over the course of two years, Warren's condition improved only slightly. He had to learn to walk again, and he was moved to the hospital. Betty visited him after work. Warren's return to health, however, did not change Betty's mind. A terse two-sentence statement in her memoirs serves to explain the end of the relationship: "Then, miraculously, Bill recovered. As soon as he was all right, back at work again, and could take care of himself, I went to a lawyer and started divorce proceedings." Those proceedings were concluded in September 1947. She would later tell an interviewer, "I took a dollar in settlement and it was finished." Her mother and stepfather welcomed her back into their home, where she stayed for a few months until she once again took her own apartment.[26]

On the surface, Betty's treatment of Warren in the last years of their relationship seems rather cold and callous. Indeed, she makes no attempt to spin any warmth into the situation. One explanation may be that she had finally found what she wanted, and with the single-minded determination that would distinguish her character for her entire life, went after it at the first possible moment. But an alternative explanation can be found in the couple's divorce decree, filed in the records of the Michigan Board of Health. On it, the court listed the "Cause for Which Divorced" as "extensive repeated cruelty." Certainly if that was the case, Betty was well justified in acting as she did. For her part, Betty has made little mention of her first marriage, and no mention of the details of her relationship with Warren, save this cryptic comment in her memoirs: "I didn't fail, but it's a long time ago and nothing's gained by going into the details."[27]

In the space of five years, Betty Bloomer Warren, trained dancer and professional woman, had gone from a party girl, to a short-lived engagement, to a five-year marriage to a salesman who, like her father, was an alcoholic, and, unlike her father, may well have abused her. Indeed, her life put her at high risk for alcoholism, and she was beginning to show signs of the disease in her behavior. And yet she had developed into an independent professional woman—far more independent than was the norm in the postwar period. Although she had not been a "Rosie the Riveter" during the war, neither had she retreated into her parents' home and waited for a soldier to come home. She had taught, had worked in an executive position, and had helped nurse an invalid husband back to health. By 1947, she had had enough and was ready to find a less complicated life. But "settling down" was a relevant term. For most women who had worked in the nation's factories during the war, marriage and family were the goals, as women moved to achieve the stability in their lives that had eluded their own mothers since at least 1929. But for Betty, the goal was now to pursue the career of a fashion buyer. She had hoped that Warren would be the father of her children; now, she had no illusions about achieving a domestic lifestyle. Indeed, she was absolutely adamant: "I was so fed up with marriage that I knew I'd never consider another one."[28]

CHAPTER 2

"THE CONGRESS GOT A MINORITY LEADER, AND I LOST A HUSBAND"

The man who would become Betty's second husband was born in Omaha, Nebraska, on July 14, 1913, as Leslie Lynch King. His father physically abused his mother to the point that she gathered up her child, divorced her husband, and moved back to her parent's home in Grand Rapids, Michigan. There she married Gerald R. Ford Sr., a paint and varnish salesman who gave her son his name. "Junior" Ford, as he was called by family and friends alike, led an idyllic midwestern life. He was an Eagle Scout and a star football player both in high school and at the University of Michigan. One friend remembered that he was their "hero" in high school—"it was like Gary Cooper and Jerry Ford." The handsome Ford (who, like his future wife, would as a youth earn money as a fashion model) decided not to entertain offers to play professional football, and instead he attended Yale University Law School, where he graduated in 1941. He returned to Grand Rapids to set up a law firm with his friend Philip Buchen, only to have his plans deferred, along with millions of other young men, by Pearl Harbor. Ford's service in the navy during World War II almost cost him his life, as he came close to being swept off the deck of the *USS Monterey* during a typhoon. He returned to Grand Rapids in 1946, rejoined his law firm, and immediately entered local politics.[1]

Ford first met Betty Warren at a cocktail party sometime in 1947. He remembered that after that meeting, two mutual friends, Peg and Jim Neuman, suggested that he call Betty, then in the process of obtaining her divorce from Bill Warren, and ask her for a date. He later recalled: "she was younger than I was, she'd gone to a different high school, and I didn't know her well. Still I remembered how attractive she was, and I knew she was one of Peg's best friends." There was much working against a relationship. Both had busy schedules, and her divorce was still pending. Thus, a date would, in the mores of the day, easily be interpreted as an affair. Betty was hesitant; Ford was persistent; Betty finally acquiesced. Their first date was, as Ford remembers it, at "an out of the way bar." There was an immediate attraction; as Ford coolly put it, "my interest [was] piqued."[2]

The courtship progressed slowly. Betty's divorce was not final until September 1947, so the couple had to take care of their reputations. And even after the divorce, the couple continued to see other people, and agreed, at least for the moment, that marriage was not in the cards. Betty had even considered moving to Brazil to work in the fashion industry. Yet Betty also had another reason for exercising some caution. She initially believed that Ford was still in love with his first serious romance, a New York model named Phyllis Brown. Whether or not that is true is a matter for conjecture. Nevertheless, in a moment that was either naive, insensitive, or both, Ford suggested that during a buying trip to New York City, Betty look up his old flame. She did so, and Brown humiliated Betty, making fun of her midwestern accouterments. Betty would later tell an interviewer: "Phyllis is a nice lady. She just didn't want to live in Grand Rapids." But according to a Ford biographer, the episode "almost busted up the romance."[3]

However, the most important distraction was politics. Ford's folksy charm masked a man whose political ambitions always ran deep. These ambitions almost ended his relationship with Betty before it had really begun. Ford had decided to run for the House of Representatives from Michigan's Fifth Congressional District, and to do so, he would have to mount a primary challenge against Bartel Jonkman, a four-term incumbent. Ford's two closest advisers, law partner Phil Buchen and friend Jack Stiles, had told him that he should keep the element of surprise in his announcement, and not even tell Betty. Their reasoning was simple—they were convinced that marrying a woman who was both a professional dancer and a divorcée would cost Ford votes among the Calvinistic Dutch in his district. As one Ford adviser later told a biographer, "with Jonkman being Dutch, why we just couldn't risk that kind of bad publicity."[4]

But Ford was adamant. He wanted a political career and Betty, too. The two principals disagree on when Ford actually proposed marriage. She remembers it as the fall of 1947; he remembers it being February 1948. Both agree, however, that when he finally popped the question, he hedged it with the bombshell that they could not be immediately married, and he could not tell her why. When he finally told her of his plans, he made it clear that because he had decided to run for Congress, their relationship could not be made public. Indeed, they could not be married until at least after the primary (Jonkman lived right up the street from Betty, and discovery was always a concern), and as close to the general election as was practically possible. In the fall, running against a Democrat in a strongly Republican district, Ford would have much less to worry about. When he sprung all this on his new fiancée, as he later, somewhat ruefully, remembered, "that didn't sit too well, as you can imagine."[5]

The couple was officially engaged in July 1948. Two months later, Ford beat Jonkman by a plurality of some 9,300 votes. On October 15, two weeks before the general election, he and Betty were married. Her wedding dress was paid for with fifty dollars that her fiancé had won on a bet. (A supporter bet Ford that he would not carry Ottawa County in the primary. Ford did.) The night before the ceremony, Ford left the rehearsal dinner early to make a campaign speech, leaving the bride to dine with the minister. On the day of the wedding, the groom was late—and wearing brown, mud-soiled shoes with a dark suit—because he had been campaigning right up to the last minute (Figure 2.1). The newlyweds left for their honeymoon with the best man in the car, and drove to Ann Arbor so that they could attend a University of Michigan football game. (Ford went to the game alone, however, as his exhausted bride stayed in the hotel room.) Then they drove to Owosso, Michigan, to hear presidential candidate Thomas Dewey—himself born in Owosso—speak. On their return that night to Grand Rapids, Betty remembered that her new husband announced, "I've got a very important political meeting at 7:30. Do you suppose you could fix me a sandwich before I leave?"[6]

Figure 2.1. Wedding day, October 15, 1948. Left to right: Gerald R. Ford Sr.,
Dorothy Gardner Ford; Gerald R. Ford Jr., Betty Ford, Hortense Neahr Bloomer
Godwin, and Arthur Meigs Godwin (courtesy of the Gerald R. Ford Library).

Betty Ford later remembered "when I married Jerry Ford, I really thought I was marrying a lawyer, and he would practice law until it was time for him to retire, and we would spend the quiet life of a medium-sized city in Grand Rapids, Michigan." This statement rings as disingenuous. By the time they married, it was crystal clear that Gerald Ford was a politician with national ambitions, hardly a small-town lawyer. And despite her protest that "I was very unprepared to be a political wife, but I didn't worry because I didn't think he was going to win"—win he did. That November, Ford easily outpolled his Democratic rival. And thus Betty Bloomer Warren Ford, late a professional buyer for a large department store, once a professional educator and dancer, now found herself a congressman's wife.[7]

Just as important, she would be without the person who had shaped her early life. On November 20, 1948, only days after Ford's electoral victory, Betty's mother, Hortense Neahr Bloomer Godwin, died at her Hollywood, Florida, home. The causes were listed as ptomaine poisoning and a cerebral hemorrhage. Mrs. Ford's mother was buried four days later in Kalamazoo, Michigan.[8]

* * *

Ford's preoccupation with his congressional campaign was but a portent of things to come. His sister Janet was prophetic when she warned her new sister-in-law that "you won't have to worry about other women. Jerry's *work* will be the other woman." To say that Ford threw himself into his work is to seriously understate his zeal. A workaholic with a rare gift for making politics look both easy and fun, Ford mastered the complexities of legislative life, while at the same time earning the respect of all those around him. Of particular interest to him were budgetary matters, and as a member of the House Appropriations Committee, one of the most powerful and busy committees in Congress, his time was at a premium. With his star rising, in 1960, Ford's name was floated by Republican presidential nominee Richard Nixon for the vice presidency. The following year, the American Political Science Association named him "Congressman's Congressman." It was to be one of the most cherished awards of his career. In December 1963, in testament to the respect with which he was held on both sides of the aisle, Ford was chosen by Lyndon Johnson to be the sole Republican legislator to serve on the Warren Commission, which investigated the assassination of President John F. Kennedy.[9]

Ford now sought leadership roles for himself. In 1964, in the wake of the resonant defeat of Barry Goldwater for the presidency, House Republicans quivered for a change. Younger members ousted the old leadership and narrowly elected the fifty-four-year-old Ford as minority whip. The following year, the same Republican insurgents led a successful coup against Charles Halleck of Indiana, and elected Ford to the post of minority leader, thus making him the second most powerful member in the House. Ford and his counterpart in the Senate, minority leader Everett Dirksen of Illinois, made a particularly effective team. Weekly television appearances, dubbed "The Ev and Jerry Show," not only galvanized the loyal opposition after the Goldwater debacle, but also exposed the likable, engaging, and telegenic Ford to the nation. In 1968, he was now seriously considered by the Nixon team for the vice presidency. He was only passed over because of the hope that if the Republicans won a majority that fall, the Nixon team felt that he would make a compliant Speaker of the House. However, Nixon's razor-thin victory did not carry with it a Republican majority. Four years later, more concerned with destroying the token opposition of George McGovern than with helping fellow Republicans, Nixon won in a landslide, but his party was still in the minority in Congress, and Ford continued to serve as his party's leader in the House.[10]

Betty Ford did those things expected of a wife of a member of Congress who was on the fast track to power. She met constituents for tours, helped out in the office on weekends (Ford quietly inquired as to whether or not she could be paid, but soon dropped the idea), and became active in the "Congressional Club"—a bipartisan group of legislative, Supreme Court, and cabinet wives. In her own eyes, Mrs. Ford believed that she "behaved like a typical congressional wife." Yet this assessment was far too humble. Although there was never any thought of her staking her own claim in what in the 1950s was chiefly a man's world, as she told biographer James Cannon, "I saw that I would have to grow with Jerry, or be left behind. And I had *no* intention of being left behind." Along with her more traditional, expected duties, she set out to learn as much as she could about her husband's new trade. She researched the job of a congressman in the Library of Congress and spent time in the House galleries watching the debates, so that she might learn the intricacies of her husband's second home. Once, she did something that is the bane of every high school student of government, and apparently did it with zest and interest. She tracked the progress of one bill all the way through its path in the House—from introduction on the floor, to committee, to vote.[11]

Betty Ford was a quick study. But more important, she had an instinct for the game that made her one of the most politically astute women in Washington. Once, she told a Republican congressman's wife to participate in the ladies' fashion shows because all the wives of the Democratic members did, and the other side should not be allowed to hog the camera. Her husband later paid his wife what was, for him, a high compliment: "Although she never enjoyed politics, she had a good ear and a remarkable sensitivity for the nuances of what was happening." By her own admission, she had begun her husband's career not being quite sure she was as devoted to it as was he, but that was changing. As one close observer noted, she had learned that she was "not without ambition for her husband."[12]

Yet Mrs. Ford wanted more than politics in her life; she wanted a stability that she had yet to know with either her father or her first husband. A particular target of her attention was her husband's roving eye; in fact, he was known then and throughout his public career as a gentleman whose head was easily turned by a beautiful woman. But this was something that his wife never accepted passively. She remembered in a 1984 interview that while Ford went to Washington as a married man, he was "still thought of as an attractive young bachelor." As she recalled: "the invitations that came to his office usually were addressed just to him. After sitting home by myself for some of those first events and hearing about them from other wives the next day, I really had to step in and sort of put my foot down."[13]

Security could also be gained by starting a family. And yet, one could almost hear her sigh as she told an interviewer: "We had three boys and a girl over seven years. That was perhaps more than I expected." On March 14, 1950, their first son, Michael, was born. Two years later, almost to the day, on March 16, 1952, a second son, Jack, was born (in the interim, Mrs. Ford had a miscarriage). On May 19, 1956, Steven was born, and Susan Elizabeth was born on July 6 of the following year.[14]

With a growing family came several changes in address. Immediately after his election, Ford rented a one-bedroom apartment on Q Street in Georgetown. The Fords lived there until June 1951, when they moved across the river and rented a two-bedroom apartment in Alexandria. They grew to love the Virginia suburb; in 1955, they built a two-story home on Crown View Drive. It would remain the Ford's home for the next twenty years—their next one would be on 1600 Pennsylvania Avenue.[15]

And yet stability continued to elude Betty Ford. As her husband's career blossomed, and as he became more and more respected as both a legislator and as a campaigner—particularly for his stump-speaking abilities, which were always without peer—he traveled more and more. By his own admission, "even as a junior member of the House, I was on the road constantly, and it was difficult to establish a patterned presence at home." After becoming minority leader, in 1966 alone, he made two hundred speaking trips.[16]

In an interview with the author, son Jack Ford observed, "I never really felt like it was a single-parent house. When he was home, he was really home." These feelings had been echoed some thirty years before by his sister Susan, when she made light of her father's absences to *Time* magazine: "Dad really just wasn't home a lot, so when he was there, it was so special we did everything we could to make him happy—and he did everything he could to make us happy." However, this attitude masked a resentment that lay just below the surface of life in the Ford household. Four years later, in a quote solicited by Betty for inclusion in the first volume of her memoirs, Susan spoke less charitably of her father's absences: "I love my father, but I didn't know I had a father until I was 10 or 12 years old. Everybody was supposed to be home for dinner Sunday night because Daddy always made a point of being home for Sunday-night dinner. Well, it meant nothing to me. Just a man sitting there at the table." Indeed, at the moment that Susan was born, Ford was fulfilling a long-made promise to his sons and was with them at a Washington Senators baseball game.[17]

As a little girl, Betty Bloomer had vowed that she would never marry a man who, like her father, traveled constantly. And now she had not only done so—she had done so twice. Some years later, Betty Ford was to recall a Drew Pearson article that mentioned that the "Gerald Ford's were in the Far East." With some bitterness, she remarked, "Gerald Ford was in the Far East, but I was right here, chauffeuring and cooking." She later remembered for *Vogue* magazine that her husband was so often gone, one night when she turned over in her sleep, she saw him sleeping beside her and quipped, "What are *you* doing here?"[18]

It is difficult, and perhaps not particularly useful, to try to assess whether this was neglect on Ford's part. Theirs was a classic suburban relationship of the 1950s. He had a career and growing influence; she was the supportive wife; and together, they made a virtually unbeatable team. But Mrs. Ford's oft-quoted remark, that in 1965 "the Congress got a new Minority Leader, and I lost a husband," misses the point widely. The year 1965 saw no real watershed in the construction of their relationship. She had never had a full-time husband, and her children had never had a full-time father. For his part, however, Ford remembers, "personally, Betty and I were as happy as we could possibly be." This is no doubt a sincere belief. But as Ford made his move to grasp his share of power in the House, a series of domestic shocks served to challenge that notion.[19]

Immediately after the 1964 Republican convention, Betty Ford suffered a serious health crisis. After having trouble raising a window, she experienced a pain in her left arm and an accompanying swelling in her hand horrifying enough to warrant her being taken to the emergency room of the National Orthopedic Hospital. The diagnosis was a pinched nerve in her neck, ruled to be an inoperable condition because no operable lesion was found. Hot towels, massage, cortisone shots, yoga, injections of gold salts, even traction—nothing alleviated the excruciating pain. Indeed, there were periods of partial paralysis. To make matters even worse, during her therapy, she also developed a severe case of osteoarthritis. A variety of the disease—that which afflicted Mrs. Ford, and which occurs most often in older women—attacks women in their forties, and involves the bony protuberances over the joints of the fingers and toes. Throughout the rest of her life, she would have to cope with swollen fingers, knobby knuckles, and a misshapen thumb. Even after her dismissal from the hospital, the pain did not subside. As a result, and of critical importance for her future, her doctors began to prescribe increasing doses of pain-killing drugs. But the pain continued. It was soon seen that the only thing that stood to offer respite from the pain would be to decrease the level of tension in her life—something that was not about to happen to the wife of a member of Congress who was bent on achieving a leadership position. Years of being a single parent, years of managing a household and children largely on her own, and months of pain were about to take their toll.[20]

As the wife of a successful politician, Betty Ford struggled with the same demons that plagued many suburban housewives in the 1950s. With an absentee husband and a growing family, she served as primary caregiver, struggling not to lose herself in the process. In 1963, in her masterpiece *The Feminine Mystique*, Betty Friedan identified those demons for the first time: "It was a strange stirring, a sense of dissatisfaction. . . . Each suburban wife struggled with it alone. . . . We can no longer ignore that voice within women that says, 'I want something more than my husband and my children and my home.'"

As did many of the women described by Friedan as having what she termed "The Problem That Has No Name," Mrs. Ford turned to alcohol and drugs to ease the pain of being alone.[21]

Betty Ford had lived in a family and led a life that made her a high-risk candidate for alcoholism. Marrying Gerald Ford did little to lessen that risk—and much to increase it. He was absent as much as her father and first husband had been. Moreover, she had been taken from a life in Grand Rapids where, as she remembered, she had "the pleasure of being looked upon as a leader in my own community. And losing that caused some buried resentment." Despite her husband's success, and the role she had played in achieving that success, she was unhappy with her lot in life in 1965, perhaps even more so than she had been in 1945. She felt that she had "lost [her] feeling of self-worth." Mrs. Ford observed in the second volume of her memoirs, "I just don't remember when I went from being a social drinker to being preoccupied with drinking, but I'm sure it was pretty gradual." Perhaps. But there is little doubt as to what sparked her "preoccupation." As she later admitted, "I was feeling terribly neglected . . . the loneliness . . . makes liquor more attractive." By 1964, Mrs. Ford remembered that she had begun mixing her alcohol with her painkillers.[22]

Finally, for the first time in her life, Betty Ford screamed for help. About one year after her mother had pinched her nerve, eight-year-old Susan found her sobbing so uncontrollably that she had the family housekeeper call her father, who was then on the presidential yacht *Sequoia,* talking with President Johnson about the course of the Vietnam War. Ford raced home; when he arrived, he found their family doctor. He told Ford that his wife should see a psychiatrist. She had clearly had a nervous breakdown (Susan remembered, "she *did* want to take me and run away"), but it was one that she would keep secret until the writing of the second volume of her memoirs in 1987 (telling a reporter in 1974 that "no one had a nervous breakdown. If anything broke down, it was that nerve in my neck"). Following this incident, Mrs. Ford began to see a psychiatrist. (Ford saw the psychiatrist as well, but his wife did not want them to go together.) Of her treatment, she remembered, "He told me to believe I was important, and that if I went to pieces I wouldn't be of much value to Jerry or the children." Later, she tried to make light of it—"There wasn't anything terribly wrong with me. I just wasn't the Bionic Woman." Yet the counseling did not solve the larger problem in her life, as she continued to mix her cocktails and painkillers.[23]

According to Ford's brother Tom, "Jerry had a guilt complex" about his wife's health. He remembered that his brother would "inconvenience himself and stay home from speaking engagements, he'd bring her gifts and pitch in to help in every way he could." Yet even if this was true, it was hardly enough. Aside from these tokens of attention, the ambitious Ford simply turned a deaf ear to his wife's problem. The same was true of her children. There is no record—or mention by any of the principals involved—of the family trying to get help for Betty before they finally intervened in 1978 (see Chapter 6). As son Mike later put it, "No one really wanted to admit that we were watching our mother change. . . . We were in denial." Indeed, despite growing evidence that his wife was seriously ill, it took eight more years before Ford first discussed with his wife the possibility of his retirement. In 1973, he finally promised her that he would get out of politics in 1977, after the next presidential election. It was a promise that Ford would keep, but not for the reasons he originally believed.[24]

By the spring of 1973, Vice President Spiro T. Agnew was in trouble. A Maryland grand jury was deciding whether he should be indicted for tax evasion, bribery, and extortion schemes carried out while he was governor of Maryland. According to two *Washington Post* reporters, on Saturday, October 6, White House Chief of Staff Alexander Haig called in speechwriter Patrick Buchanan and told him to add a new ending to the Watergate speech that he was writing. At the end of the speech, Nixon would announce Agnew's resignation. Four days later, Agnew resigned.[25]

Hours before Agnew's resignation, Nixon met with Ford. Now bound by the Twenty-fifth Amendment to nominate a candidate for the vice presidency subject to the approval of Congress, he asked Ford to coordinate recommendations from Republican members of Congress, and told him that he wanted those recommendations by 6:00 PM the following day. After Ford left, Nixon spoke with advisers Bryce Harlow and Melvin Laird, and Speaker of the House Carl Albert. All three men told the president that regardless of the president's druthers (his first choice for his nominee was Secretary of the Treasury John Connally), Ford was the only confirmable choice. Later that evening, before he even saw the results of the recommendations, Nixon instructed Laird to call Ford to sound him out about the nomination.[26]

Laird called Ford at his home to ask him if he would accept the vice presidential nomination if he was asked. Ford said that he would. The next day in the Oval Office, Nixon formally offered Ford the nomination. Ford accepted, and he made it clear that he did not expect to be the party's standard-bearer in 1976. Nixon's response was blunt: "Well, that's good, because John Connally is my choice for 1976." Ford tells the story that when Nixon called his home later that night to discuss the details of the announcement, he had to ask him to call back on the listed number so that Mrs. Ford could listen in on an extension. She later remembered, "Susan had bet me five dollars that the President would choose Jerry to replace Agnew, and I lost the bet."[27]

Two hours after that phone call, Nixon announced his choice to the nation. Clearly reveling in the fact that few of those assembled in the East Room had learned of his decision, the president tried to drag out the drama of the moment. But when he said that his choice had twenty-five years of experience in the House, noticeable smiles came over the faces of the audience. When the melodramatic Nixon finally announced Ford's name, the room went wild with cheering and whistling. Clearly astonished, Nixon turned to Ford and whispered, "They like you." Ford then briefly addressed his audience, saying that he was "terribly humbled," and that "I hope I have some assets that might be helpful in working with Congress."[28]

No one had apparently thought that Mrs. Ford would join the dais. There was no chair for her, and she had to share Pat Nixon's chair. When the ceremony was over, Nixon turned to her to offer his congratulations. "Congratulations or condolences?" she quipped. According to Ford speechwriter Robert T. Hartmann, who witnessed the exchange, "Nixon smiled but had no answer."[29]

Time magazine saw the nomination in a positive light: "Gerald Ford has the immense asset of a corruption-free reputation. He has a solid if unimaginative record in domestic policy, stands somewhere near the American center, and is greatly liked and respected on Capitol Hill." But for the most part, a press that had been made cynical by Vietnam and Watergate was wary about praising the vice president designate. A *Washington Post* editorial called him "pedestrian, partisan, dogged—he has been the very model of a second-level party man." The *New York Times* sniffed that Ford was "a routine partisan of narrow views." Yet in an interesting irony, both these editorials put their finger on the reason that Ford was chosen by Nixon—his history of party loyalty had made him few enemies and would almost guarantee his confirmation.[30]

Despite all its public cheering, Congress was wary, too. Although respect for Ford ran deep on both sides of the aisle and in both chambers, public suspicion of the presidency was at a fever pitch in October 1973. Ford would be the first to test the succession provision of the Twenty-fifth Amendment, and no one assumed that his confirmation hearings would be a breeze. Ford remembered, "some 350 special agents from 33 of the Bureau's field offices . . . interviewed more than 1,000 witnesses and compiled 1,700 pages of reports." And this investigation was not aimed at illuminating his qualifications for the job. Rather, the overwhelming majority of the questions probed Ford's personal life and his views on Nixon's fate. Ford's views on policy were virtually ignored.[31]

Along with every other part of his personal life, Ford's finances were scrupulously inspected. As a result, his wife was also dragged into the process. A psychiatrist named Robert Winter-Berger appeared as a witness and charged that between 1966 and 1969, he had loaned Ford some $15,000. According to Winter-Berger, the money was used to help pay for Mrs. Ford's hospitalization for an illness of the pancreas. In the margins of a memo on the subject, Ford penned: "No truth . . . Blue Cross/Blue Shield." Winter-Burger's testimony was soon exposed as being so contradictory that the committee considered charging him with perjury. The four different votes confirming Ford's nomination were overwhelmingly positive. The Senate Rules Committee supported him, 9–0. The House Judiciary Committee voted 24–8 nine days later. In the full House, the vote was 387–35, and in the Senate, it was 92–3. Democrats cast all of the nay votes.[32]

Ford requested that he be sworn in at the Capitol. Nixon de-
murred, stating his preference for a White House ceremony (an aide
told Hartmann that Nixon was afraid that he would be booed when
he walked down the center aisle with Ford). But Ford persisted, and
Nixon finally agreed. His December 6, 1973, speech to Congress and
the nation after being sworn was the first vice presidential inaugural
address to include a tribute to his wife, who was, as Ford noted,
"standing by my side, as she always has."[33]

Son Steve remembered that his mother "didn't want to go
there. . . . She had Dad retired. . . . But history came in, snapped its
fingers, and ruined her plans." Yet according to biographer James
Cannon, Mrs. Ford thought that life was going to be easier for their
family once Ford settled into the vice presidency. If, indeed, she believed this, she would immediately be disappointed. The promotion
of Ford to vice president only increased his time away from home.
The new second lady joked, "I like to travel too, but not the way
Jerry does it. He feels he's got to go up and down as many times as
the airplane can stop." During his eight months in office, Ford visited forty states, giving some five hundred speeches. Writer Norman
Mailer quipped, "Somebody ought to do Jerry Ford a favor and take
his airplane away from him."[34]

A globe-trotting vice president, who most observers believed
would occupy the Oval Office in a matter of months, Gerald Ford
was hardly the average American dad. And yet the nation chose to
accept his as the quintessential American family. The country, Watergate weary, wanted normalcy as fast as it could get it, and it initially reveled in the seeming midwestern simplicity of their new
Second Family. It ignored the fact that it was peering at the powerful
and observing one of the most visible families in the world, and instead it embraced the hope that there might still be people like
themselves in government. They were portrayed, and accepted, not
as the Washington insiders that Ford and his family had actually become, but as the family of the heartland—the Grand Rapids Fords.

The press, particularly the traditional women's magazines, was a
willing accomplice in portraying the Fords as the embodiment of
small-town Americana from the moment that Ford had been confirmed as vice president. In the May 1974 issues of *Good Housekeeping* and *McCall's,* the nation learned that the Fords of Grand Rapids

took family drives in a 1969 Chrysler, that after a family vote they decided to stay in Alexandria rather than actually live in the newly acquired home for the vice president at Observatory Place, and that they had made security improvements on their Alexandria home at their own expense, writing their neighbors to apologize for the confusion in the neighborhood. *Good Housekeeping* observed that they were "a beautiful family, no question about that," and gushed: "Are these people real? Is such perfection possible in this very imperfect world? With their good looks, good health, good fortune, their hard work, their devout prayers, the Gerald Fords do come miraculously close to embodying our collective fantasy of the family folks next door."[35]

For their part, *McCall's*—which entitled their story "The Closest Family in Washington"—paid them what was perhaps the ultimate American compliment, when it compared the Fords to television's most successful family: "If Betty Ford . . . sounds like something out of an old 'Father Knows Best' episode, the impression is not far off the mark. The Fords do have a marked resemblance to the happy, wholesome families that populate the television series." But the mother of this family was about to break with tradition.[36]

There was no hint of public activism in Betty Ford before she met Gerald Ford. Although she was both outspoken and a professional woman, she showed no hint of advocating any cause outside of her own career. There was no clue that she took social or political stands of any kind before 1947. Even after meeting Ford, she did not campaign by his side as a partner. Much of this was because, as a divorcée, she could not do so without raising conservative eyebrows. But a large part of it was, as she later noted when referring to presidential politics in 1948, "I couldn't have been less interested." She was concerned about politics and causes only as they affected her husband's career. Throughout his congressional tenure, she never once publicly advocated a cause in a speech or a statement. Indeed, she was so nervous about speaking in public that she joined twelve other political wives in taking a speech course. Primarily content to be a mother and a wife, Betty Ford had, by choice, renounced a career as a professional woman and chosen instead the dual roles of homemaker and political partner. And by their very definition in the two decades after World War II, both these roles kept the women who chose them out of the spotlight.[37] However, it is clear that after Ford was named vice president, a change came over his wife. Slowly, she was beginning to revert back to the woman she had been before she married Gerald Ford—a self-assured woman of candor who enjoyed the spotlight. James Cannon sagely observed that as a professional performer—a dancer—Betty Ford naturally gravitated to a stage. There was no such stage on which the wife of a congressman could perform. But after 1973, when she suddenly became an internationally known figure, she blossomed. As Cannon put it: "she was a performer—the spotlight shines on her, she performs." The artist in Betty Ford had just been waiting to come out. Perhaps her mentor Martha Graham put it best when asked to describe her most famous student: "Part of the training of a dancer is to meet a situation with courage and the necessity for complete honesty." An interviewer noted that she had a "strong sense of self . . . assertive, self-assured, and confident." Others noticed the same change. Jane Howard, in the *New York Times Magazine,* likened the transformation to that of Cinderella: "Onstage again, after 26 years of wifely obscurity and motherly sacrifice, it was as if she was picking up where she left off when she said good-by [*sic*] to Martha Graham."[38]

As a result, the traditional role of the second lady was much too confining for Mrs. Ford. She showed the expected deference and reticence throughout her husband's confirmation process. She immediately announced that art and dance would be her pet projects. Also, she announced that she would undertake the redecorating of the Admiralty House at Observatory Place. As the wife of the vice president, she automatically became the president of Red Cross Wives, a role that was deliberately low profile. However, she surprised the nation by not limiting herself to low-profile causes. Despite opposition from Nixon's staff, Betty insisted on volunteering to go to Atlanta representing the administration at the funeral of Martin Luther King Jr.'s mother, who had been shot while playing the organ at the Ebenezer Baptist Church. She went, and then–Georgia governor Jimmy Carter helped with the arrangements. She also showed a spirit of candor on the issue of women's rights. One example of this was a speech given at the Women's Center for

Life-Long Learning at Utah State University on June 8, 1974. In this address, Mrs. Ford claimed that a "third of [women] are the sole wage earners in their household," a fact that she decried as "one of our country's biggest problems." She then listed the discrepancy of pay for professional women ("even in a field where they should be almost equal—college and university teaching—women are paid seventeen percent less than their male colleagues"), a problem that she placed on the shoulders of "our whole society, *not* just the individual woman."[39]

Mrs. Ford was also remarkably candid with the press, displaying an openness that was certainly novel but that often seemed to border on the indiscreet. In an interview given to *McCall's* magazine, she was outspoken about what her reaction would be if one of her children admitted to using marijuana: "I'd be understanding. I would object and try to reason with them rather than try to use force." And in *Good Housekeeping,* she said that she agreed with the Supreme Court's 1973 decision in *Roe v. Wade,* which legalized abortion through the second trimester of pregnancy. ("I'm glad abortion has been taken out of the back rooms and put into the hospitals where it belongs.") This latter statement drew the most attention— and irate constituent mail—of any statement made by the second lady. But she did not back down. As she told interviewer Barbara Hower in summer 1974: "The people who wrote couldn't understand that I wasn't advocating abortion as a form of birth control. I just feel that medically safe operations are better than back-alley butcher jobs. Having babies is a blessing, not a duty."[40]

Betty Ford was certainly different. But this should not be read to mean that she was an Eleanor Roosevelt–like advocate for ideas, stumping to convince the public of her opinions. Not yet, anyway. While second lady, Betty had many reasons to wish to be seen in public as little as possible. Although some reporters obliquely referred to her health, few if any were aware during the vice presidential period of the depth of her fragility. No stories were printed that speculated on a drinking problem; few referred to her as anything but candid and honest. But this was a woman suffering from three diseases—arthritis, alcoholism, and addiction to painkillers—all of which sapped her strength. She was often in traction for her arthritis, and she had a spur on her foot removed during the vice presidential period. Indeed, an Alexandria neighbor told a reporter on the night her husband was chosen to replace Agnew that Mrs. Ford "has a malfunction of some kind"—follow-up on this comment did not appear in the press.[41]

Ford was not unaware of his wife's growing problems, particularly with alcohol. Before becoming president, he talked about the dilemma with Bill Bloomer. Ford reassured his brother-in-law that "If it gets serious, we'll do something." Yet in retrospect, this was hardly enough. As Cannon carefully put it, "in his preoccupation with his work and solving the problem of a vast government, Ford did not see the problem that was developing in his own home." Like Hortense with Betty's father, Ford was now fulfilling the role of the classic enabler—his passive attitude toward his wife's health crises, and his shielding of his wife from the consequences of her actions by making jokes about her tardiness and absences from social obligations were feeding the disease that was controlling his wife.[42]

At one point during her husband's vice presidency, Mrs. Ford came perilously close to telling the world of her addictions. She had been asked to represent the Nixon Administration at the first stop of the Art Train, a six-car museum that went to areas of the country that had no museums. She joined the train in Georgia, where the then–first lady of the state, Rosalynn Carter, hosted her. A haggard-looking Mrs. Ford was asked by a reporter if she was "on something." In the caboose of Art Train, the second lady admitted that she took a Valium per day; a White House clarification was issued to make it clear that it was for her pinched nerve.[43]

This was a woman in pain; this was a woman who sorely needed a friend. Nancy Howe served this purpose. Howe, a native of Lynchburg, Virginia, had graduated from Anderson Junior College in South Carolina and from Lynchburg College. After her marriage to James Howe, an army officer, she lived at posts in the United States, Japan, and Panama. By 1972, he had retired from the army, and he taught Spanish and chaired the Department of Modern Languages at Trenton State College, commuting to his job from their Washington home and returning on the weekends. To fill her days, Howe got a job at the White House Historical Association Bookshop, selling guidebooks to people touring the White House, a job that she had gotten through her daughter, Lise Courtney, who had worked at the bookshop as a summer job. In the summer of 1973, the bookshop found itself in need of another employee. Lise Courtney, who had attended Holton Arms prep school in Washington, called her alma mater to see if they could recommend someone for the job. They did—Holton Arms junior Susan Ford.

Susan and Lise Courtney became fast friends, often visiting at each other's homes and keeping in touch when each returned to school that fall (Susan to Holton Arms, Lise Courtney to law school at William and Mary). On October 12, 1973, the day that Gerald Ford was nominated to the vice presidency, Howe remembered that Susan called her "first thing." Howe volunteered her services in case there was anything that the family needed to have done. When Howe went to the Ford's Alexandria home to deliver an anniversary present to the Fords, she found it a madhouse of ringing phones and unannounced visitors. She once again offered her services to help straighten out the pandemonium. The next day, she was working for the Fords on a full-time basis. For her part, Howe gushed of Betty, "She's the most special person I've ever known. I feel as if I should give her back my paycheck at the end of the month."[44]

For all intents and purposes, Howe moved into the Ford home in Alexandria and filled a gap that had long been present in Betty Ford's life—that of a companion. Howe found a kindred spirit in the second lady, with whom she shared a love of the arts, specifically the ballet. Howe was originally hired as Mrs. Ford's appointments secretary, and she took on the task of answering her boss's mail. However, Howe quickly became Betty Ford's chief aide de camp, serving every need of the second lady, from personal shopper to doorkeeper to confidante. Soon, she was handling the scheduling of press interviews as well as answering correspondence. One writer who interviewed Mrs. Ford in Alexandria during this period marveled at both Howe's influence and the relaxed relationship that existed between her and the second lady: "[Howe] is not threatened; her authority is not in jeopardy; the two women are friends—they frequently laugh aloud together. . . . Obviously, Betty Ford is not policed." Although this latter assessment may have had a grain of truth at the beginning of the vice presidential period, it was clearly untrue toward its end. By the end of the vice presidency, Howe had become the de facto chief of staff for the second lady, deciding on appointments and controlling access to her friend. By the time the Fords entered the White House, resentment for Howe was beginning to run deep inside the Ford circle. Although neither woman seemed to sense it coming, the stage was set for what would be one of the most important turf battles of the Ford presidency.[45]

Betty Ford held no illusions that she would stay second lady for very long. Newspaperman Clifton Daniel (husband of Harry Truman's daughter Margaret) recalled attending a Washington dinner party, where the vice president and the second lady were also guests. As they reclined on chaise lounges, Daniel talked with Mrs. Ford about her efforts to refurbish the Naval Observatory. Daniel quietly asked, "Do you really think you are ever going to move into that house?" She "paused, shrugged slightly, and said nothing."[46]

On July 24, 1974, the U.S. Supreme Court announced its decision in *U.S. v. Nixon*. After weeks of angst, the court decreed that the president had to release the subpoenaed "Watergate Tapes" to Special Prosecutor Leon Jaworski. Unwilling to directly defy the court, Nixon released the tapes. They included the famous "Smoking Gun Conversation" of June 23, 1972, which showed that Nixon had ordered the CIA to impede the FBI's investigation of the Watergate break-in—a clear obstruction of justice. Three days after the court handed down its decision, the House Judiciary Committee turned out its first article of impeachment. By Monday, August 5, Ford was convinced: "Nixon was finished." Three days later, after meeting with Ford, Nixon spoke to the nation and became the first president to resign his office.[47]

Ford's wife did not mince words. After viewing Nixon's resignation speech, she was quoted as feeling "numb," like "an actor on a set, being told what to do." Yet she played her part to perfection. Once she learned from her husband of Nixon's decision, she canceled a doctor's appointment in order to shop for an appropriate dress—a signal that was not missed by the press corps. On August 9, the Fords waited for Nixon to complete his farewell address to the staff and then met them in the White House Diplomatic Reception Room. They walked the Nixons to their helicopter, *Air One*, which was waiting on the South Lawn. When Mrs. Ford expressed surprise that a red carpet had been rolled out for the occasion, a drained Pat

Figure 2.2. Inauguration of Gerald R. Ford as the thirty-eighth president of the United States. With Betty Ford and Chief Justice Warren Burger, August 9, 1974 (courtesy of the Gerald R. Ford Library).

Nixon turned and whispered, "You'll see so many of these red carpets, you'll get so you'll hate 'em." After the Nixons departed, the Fords went back inside the White House, where Chief Justice Warren Burger, who had only that day flown back in from the Netherlands for the occasion, introduced them to a packed East Room.[48]

One observer remembered that Mrs. Ford "smiled brightly" at the inauguration. Videotape of the swearing-in clearly shows that this was far from the case. Remembering that she "felt as though I were taking the oath with him, promising to dedicate my own life to the service of my country," she looked exhausted and terrified. Her eyes were glassy and her smile weak; although attentive to her husband's inaugural comments, she looked more than distant. Ford's inaugural address offered many historic firsts, not the least of which was that, as had been the case in his vice presidential address, he was the first president to make a reference to his wife—"I am indebted to no man, and to one woman, my wife." And although it may not have been a first, it certainly bears noting that she helped her husband write his speech. After being sworn in, Ford turned to his wife to kiss her and reportedly whispered "I love you"[49] (Figure 2.2). For the consumption of the press, the new first lady cooed that during the inauguration ceremony, "I really felt like I was taking that oath too." In her memoirs, she was more candid: she characterized that day quite succinctly as "the saddest day of my life."[50]

Before his administration was a month old, Ford had told reporters that he would "probably" run for his own term in 1976.

CHAPTER 3

"SHE WAS BEGINNING TO FLOWER A LITTLE"

Immediately after the inauguration, Mrs. Henry Catto, the wife of the State Department protocol officer, called the new first lady and asked, "What are you going to do about the King of Jordan?" Her husband had not been president for twenty-four hours, and they were not even living at the White House (until the mansion could be properly prepared for their arrival, the Fords were still residing at their home in Alexandria)—and Betty Ford was told that the Nixon White House had planned a state visit for King Hussein and Queen Alia of Jordan, and that a formal state dinner would be expected. Telling a reporter that "we'll just have to put on an official dinner for him . . . but he's coming a little soon on our agenda," Mrs. Ford was about to receive her trial by fire. Improvising, she worked not only with her inherited social director, Lucy Winchester, but also with friends like Peggy Stanton, the wife of a member of Congress. The result was a classic party thrown by the Fords of Grand Rapids. The royals were put up across the street from the White House at Blair House, and the formal dinner menu consisted of cold salmon, roast beef, artichoke salad, brie, and mousse. Then after dinner, the real party began, with dancing to a beat that had heretofore been absent from White House parties. Guests were treated to the president of the United States faking his way through the singing of "Bad, Bad Leroy Brown." The young queen, who would soon die in an airplane crash, gushed that it had been a "swinging party." Even the usually demure Mark Hatfield, a Republican senator from Oregon, was obviously enjoying himself, as he bellowed to no one in particular, "Happy New Year." It was August.[1]

The event epitomized what America saw in the Fords—an ease and comfort that they not only admired, but professed to see in themselves. The Fords, of course, viewed things quite differently. They had been thrust into the limelight with absolutely no time to prepare. Some seventeen years after the fact, Susan Ford remembered that unlike presidential families who had come to Washington in an aura of electoral triumph, "there was little jubilation when we moved to the White House. We were in a state of shock." While vice president, Ford had quietly tolerated the actions of a secret transition team, which had prepared several briefing books for him to use upon his eventual inauguration. That team did not concentrate at all on the role of his family or the first lady; no recommendations were made for their use within the administration until two weeks after Ford's inauguration. Thus, even more so than her husband, Betty Ford was coming into her new job without a road map.[2]

Mrs. Ford had been perfectly happy having Nancy Howe at the core of a tiny staff—indeed, during the vice presidential year, Howe was the only staffer who mattered. However, when she became first lady, she inherited Pat Nixon's entire staff. Helen McCain Smith was originally slated to continue as the first lady's press secretary, to be assisted by Terry Ivey and Patti Matson. Smith had been with the Nixon Administration since 1969 and had been named Mrs. Nixon's press secretary in 1973. But in a climate where both White House and press regarded each other not as adversaries but as enemies, everyone expected that Mrs. Ford would quickly choose her own liaison—which, as we shall see, she did with dispatch. Lucy Winchester remained as social secretary—she had held that position since the beginning of the Nixon Administration in 1969—and Susan Porter, Mrs. Nixon's appointments secretary, also kept her job.[3]

The new first lady, never an effective administrator or delegator, tried to continue to work as though she were still commanding a small staff. She drafted her own replies to her correspondence and presided over Monday afternoon staff meetings. She worked from either the Treaty Room or from a desk that had been set up in her bedroom. But the immediate tasks were too pressing—Hussein's party being but the first example of many—for the first lady to continue to act as her own chief of staff. As a result, Howe was given even more authority and responsibility. Although her formal job description continued to reflect her work with the first lady's correspondence (she answered a lot of Mrs. Ford's pro forma mail; her signature fluctuated from "Personal Assistant to Mrs. Ford," to "Special Assistant to Mrs. Ford"), her real duties, however, more closely approximated Howe's own assessment: "Whatever the First Lady needs to have done, I do." Her access to the first lady was absolute and complete. Such singular authority granted to one person created the perfect scenario for a classic Washington turf battle. From the earliest days in the White House, members of the first lady's staff grumbled about Howe's influence and power and sought allies in the West Wing for their various attempts to clip her wings.[4]

The president's staff, however, was in no shape to ride herd over the first lady's staff. Indeed, for all their pipe-smoking camaraderie, the Ford White House staff never worked well at all. Although many advisers had counseled an immediate housecleaning, Ford had little choice but to retain the services of most of Nixon's staffers. On the decision to keep Alexander Haig as chief of staff, Ford aide Robert Hartmann could only quip, "he's the one who knows how to fly the plane." Hartmann, a Ford loyalist since the vice presidency, feuded with both Haig and both his successors, Donald Rumsfeld and Dick Cheney. As the infighting intensified, Ford had to rein in his personal inclinations on staff management. Collegial by nature, the president wanted to institute a managerial style where all staffers reported to him as equals—the "spokes in a wheel" concept. But when the spokes began to feud, Ford reverted to the Eisenhower/Nixon model of staff authority: both the brusque Rumsfeld and the more reserved Cheney ultimately held total authority over the entire White House staff, both West and East Wing. But Rumsfeld's acceptance of the mantle of chief of staff only accelerated the feuding. A heavy-handed administrator, Rumsfeld did not inspire loyalty as much as fear. Even his 1975 promotion to secretary of defense, and Cheney's concurrent promotion to chief of staff, did not solve the problems; most observers felt that Rumsfeld was pulling Cheney's strings.[5]

In a White House that never got its staffing right, relations with the first lady were always an afterthought. Most importantly, the administration never formally named a liaison between the West and East Wing. In the beginning, it seems to have been understood that Hartmann, Ford's most senior aide, would assume this responsibility. However, Mrs. Ford deeply resented Hartmann's access to her husband. To reporter Myra MacPherson, she said, "perhaps I feel he oversteps his boundaries." Quietly, she let reporters know that any efforts that might reduce Hartmann's influence over her husband would be greatly appreciated. Hartmann's access indeed waned as the administration continued, but the strain remained. The next to take on the task of dealing with the first lady was Rumsfeld, largely because one of his immediate tasks was to cut the size of the East Wing staff. Neither Rumsfeld nor the first lady approached the issue in a particularly diplomatic manner. Mrs. Ford dug in, and Rumsfeld complained. Ford, most likely with a sigh, told Rumsfeld that he would have to take the cuts up with the first lady personally; the president remembered, "predictably, the size of the East Wing staff hardly changed at all."[6]

But size was less of an issue than was function. When a memo on the role of the first lady was finally prepared, it was clear from its tone that Ford's staff fully expected that the first lady would play a traditional role, one much like those of her immediate predecessors in the East Wing. It recommended that she concern herself with "guest lists and seating . . . start planning activities with the Cabinet and Sub-Cabinet wives immediately . . . occasionally walk through the residence when tours are going through . . . [and] host a picnic on the White House lawn." Betty Ford would indeed fulfill all the traditional responsibilities that had come to be expected of a first lady—what one scholar has termed her duty to be a "living lifestyle story." Her "causes"—those institutions and projects traditionally supported by the first lady—seemed conventional enough. Proclaiming that she considered her role a "twenty-four-hour-a-day volunteer job," she let it be known that she planned to continue to champion the arts (a supporter of the National Endowment of the Arts, Mrs. Ford met with Nancy Hanks, then the chairman of the NEA, to discuss projects that she could help promote) and continue her work with mentally retarded children. She worked for the organization No Greater Love, which aided children of soldiers who were missing in action, the National Heart Association, Goodwill Industries, and the American Cancer Society. She also advocated for vigilance against nursing home abuse. She even demonstrated a flair for the domestic. She and her sister-in-law Janet Ford redecorated the Oval Office. They exorcised the blue and gold, so reminiscent of Nixon's "imperial presidency," and introduced softer earth tones. But even in her public causes, there was a notable hint of independence. Many of her predecessors had helped Washington's Children's Hospital, a worthy target for largesse. However, Mrs. Ford—the woman who had taught dancing to black children in Grand Rapids—chose to concentrate her charitable efforts on the Washington Hospital for Sick Children, a hospital that served predominantly black patients. Indeed, she cajoled a family friend, New York City businessman Milton Hoffman, to donate two new rooms to the hospital.[7]

Indeed, if one assumed from her largely traditional choices of causes and her Jackie Kennedy–esque attempt to redecorate that this first lady would be neither seen nor heard, they were sorely mistaken. Since Ford had been named vice president, his wife had been slowly blossoming into an attractive public figure in her own right. She generated great copy, and she had developed during her time as the wife of the minority leader and in the more than two hundred interviews she gave as second lady a sage appreciation for the press, as well as a canny ability to work it. In one of her first interviews as first lady, Mrs. Ford—at least in the opinion of columnist George Will—"deliberately manufactured" a press opportunity where she could say that she planned to sleep with her husband "as often as possible." To some, this was a bit uncouth; to most, it was marvelous.[8]

The West Wing staff was so comfortable with the first lady's press skills that they agreed to her participation in a rather singular moment. On September 4, 1974, almost a month after her husband had taken office, Mrs. Ford gave a press conference—itself noteworthy, as it was the first given by a first lady since Mamie Eisenhower. In the East Room, seated at a table decorated with a strategically placed vase of daisies, Mrs. Ford smiled through about an hour of questioning. Looking completely at ease in front of the camera, she parried with the press with the ease of a master. When a reporter asked if she had considered what women's role would be in trying to stop future wars, the first lady smiled and deadpanned, "well, they can always enlist and make sure." She announced that she would continue her work with the arts, which she pointedly referred to as her "profession" (indeed, that evening, both she and the president attended a theater performance at the Kennedy Center, accompanied by NEA chairperson Hanks, to mark the hundredth anniversary of the National Council on the Arts), and retarded children; and that like the nation at large, her husband expected her to be able to balance the family's checkbook. She answered questions about how she would manage the family menus in a time of economic belt tightening ("we don't eat as much steak or roast beef or some of those things the boys like"). And to the laughter of the assembled scribes, she agreed to hold other press conferences "as often as I think that the press has anything to ask of interest." One point, however, would return as being eerily portent: when asked whether she would "look into the question of cancer research as soon as you can with the president to see if we can't expedite the program," the first lady quickly responded, "I'll be glad to. Only too happy."

She also proved to be able to dance her way through the land mines of the harder questions. When asked by Helen Thomas of United Press International if she was, as her son Jack had claimed, "disturbed" about her husband's announcement that he would "probably" run in 1976, Mrs. Ford claimed that she was "very surprised" at Jack's statement, but, refusing to take the bait, protested that, "two years is quite a long ways away." When pointedly asked if she would be an activist in terms of politics, she tried to have it both ways, claiming that she would "not take a political, active part in politics, as far as issues are concerned," but that she would be "happy to take a part" in the fight for the Equal Rights Amendment. And after these declarations, many of which might well have unnerved those who felt that the new first lady should, like her predecessors, be seen but not heard, she offered an olive branch. Answering a question of how she would like to be remembered as first lady, she cooed, "In a very kind way. As a constructive wife to the President."[9]

However, what was otherwise a bravura performance was largely lost in the criticism she received over one answer to one question. Asked if she supported the view of Senator James Buckley of New

York, who was advocating the view of the rising Republican right and calling for a constitutional amendment that would prohibit abortion for any reason, or the view of former New York Governor Nelson Rockefeller, recently chosen as Ford's nominee for the vice presidency and the darling of the moderate wing of the party, who favored abortion law liberalization, the first lady did not flinch: "Definitely closer to Governor Rockefeller." Despite the fact that her support for abortion rights was already a matter of public record, this answer headlined the stories of her press conference, and it elicited a flash of disapproval from conservative observers. The next day, the White House tried to spin her answer a bit more softly: Helen Smith issued a statement saying that in the cases of rape or incest, "Mrs. Ford feels abortion is certainly justified, but she definitely is not for abortion on demand." This is not what she had said. Nor was the spin consistent with her past statements on the subject, which had advocated an unlimited right for a woman to choose, thus placing her views to the left of even the moderate wing of her party. For his part, White House press secretary Jerald terHorst said that the first lady's response was "not a very definitive answer," and that her views and those of the president were "not that far apart." This was utter nonsense. Ford, an outspoken opponent of the *Roe v. Wade* decision, was poles apart from his wife on this issue. But the White House was only beginning to discover that the first lady would, when put in front of the camera, speak her mind.[10]

Criticism over Betty's first press conference, particularly her comments on abortion, might well have had a longer shelf life had it not been for the events of four days later. On September 9, Ford ended his one-month presidential honeymoon by announcing the decision that has become inexorably linked in history to the fate of his presidency. The nation was stunned when it learned that Ford had pardoned Richard Nixon for any federal crimes he "committed or may have committed or may have taken part in." In many ways, veteran White House watcher Hugh Sidey was correct when he observed, "from the moment that Ford became president, the expectations were too great. No man could live up to the hopes that grew wildly in the wake of Nixon's departure." However, in the minds of many, at the very least Ford had pardoned Nixon too early, and to some, the pardon was seen as the outgrowth of a deal between Ford and Nixon. The result was a violent outpouring of criticism in the press, the resignation of his press secretary, losses for the Republican Party in the November 1974 off-year elections, and the fanning of fires from the right wing of his party. Suddenly, Ford was no longer an average man. He was simply an average president.[11]

Betty Ford's role in the pardon of Richard Nixon remains a mystery. Betty told the press that she believed that "the president had acted in good faith" and maintained that she only knew about the pardon when Ford announced it to the country. Some sources have claimed that she advised her husband to pardon Nixon; some allege she counseled him against it. There is no primary evidence to support either claim. Ford does not mention any role for his wife in his memoirs, and for her own part, Betty simply wrote, "I'm not going to talk a lot about the pardon." Although it is difficult to conceive that Ford kept from his wife what were incredibly delicate and confidential negotiations with Nixon over the acceptance of a pardon, he did, in fact, keep the scope of those negotiations from all but a few staffers until the last possible moment.[12]

In the negative feeding frenzy that followed the announcement of the pardon, it is quite possible that the press might have attacked the first lady as well. Perhaps they would have concentrated on her rather noticeably slurring speech, or perhaps on what some had early on pointed out to be her habitual tardiness and laxness with appointments. Perhaps they might have even concentrated on some of the more candid statements that the press had let slide, like her views on abortion and women's rights. But within two weeks of the pardon, the story line had changed, as a chance medical examination brought the first phase of the Betty Ford first ladyship to an end.

Eighteen days after the announcement of the pardon, on Thursday, September 26, 1974, Mrs. Ford accompanied Nancy Howe to Bethesda Naval Hospital. Howe had scheduled an appointment for herself to get a breast cancer examination, and she had encouraged her friend to come along and follow suit. Captain Douglas Knab, the chairman of the Department of Gynecology, examined the first lady. During the course of the examination, he found a marble-sized lump in her right breast. Knab immediately called Dr. William Fouty, a navy captain who was chief of surgery at Bethesda, to examine Mrs. Ford to corroborate his findings. Fouty believed the nodule to be suspicious, and he recommended that a biopsy be performed. However, both men wanted to seek a third opinion. They notified Dr. William Lukash, the physician to the president, of their findings, and allowed the first lady to leave Bethesda without being told of their preliminary diagnosis.[13]

Back at the White House, Lukash called the president at about noon and told the president that his presence would be required at a meeting that evening at 7:00 PM. To summon the president was, as Ford remembered, a "very unusual" request; he had not even been informed of his wife's visit to the hospital that day. But the president appeared at precisely the appointed time. When he arrived, he saw both Lukash and Dr. Richard Thistlethwaite, civilian consultant for Bethesda Naval Hospital and chairman of surgery for the George Washington University Medical School. Mrs. Ford was not yet in the room—she was putting her clothes back on after Thistlethwaite's examination. In fact, she did not know that Lukash had called her husband and was surprised to see him when she emerged from the dressing room.[14]

Lukash and Thistlethwaite told the Fords what their three examinations had revealed. The doctors had indeed found a lump in her right breast, and all three of them recommended immediate surgery to determine whether it was malignant. The initial response of the first lady was to plead a full schedule, saying that "they can't operate immediately—I have a full day tomorrow" (she had agreed to take part in the groundbreaking for the Lyndon B. Johnson Memorial Grove in Virginia, and then host a reception for Lady Bird Johnson). Ford asked if twenty-four hours would make a difference; the doctors said no. The president was adamant that over the next twenty-four hours, the first lady's condition and the decision to undergo surgery would be kept secret. She would enter the hospital at the end of her commitments the following day. Then on Saturday, the doctors would perform exploratory surgery. If the lump were found to be cancerous, they would perform a mastectomy while she was still under general anesthesia. Mrs. Ford remembered that her husband "was more upset than I, I think I faced the situation rather matter-of-factly." For his part, Ford remembered "later that evening, when we went to bed, we held hands and prayed."[15]

The next day, the first lady honored her schedule. At the end of the day, she was secretly taken to Bethesda, where she was checked into the Presidential Suite (Figure 3.1). That evening, her husband, Susan, Mike, and Mike's wife Gayle joined her for dinner; Nancy Howe rarely left her side. For Gerald Ford, that night in the White House was "the loneliest night of my life."[16]

The next morning, Saturday, September 28, Mrs. Ford was awakened at 6:00 AM. She spent some time alone with Michael and Susan, and then prayed with Reverend Billy Zeoli, a close family friend and spiritual advisor. In her memoirs, Betty remembered that her entire family, including her husband, was there before she was taken to the operating room. However, other records, including Ford's memoirs, show that Ford was actually in the Oval Office as the operation began, working with Bob Hartmann on the speech he would deliver to the economic summit later that day. She was wheeled into the operating suite at precisely 7:00 AM; the surgery began one hour later, with Fouty performing the procedure. The operation was underway only fifteen minutes before a primary tumor approximately two centimeters (about the size of a quarter) in size had been removed, examined, and diagnosed as malignant.[17]

Mrs. Ford later told a reporter that "even though they said they were going to do a biopsy, I knew really that they would have to remove the breast." This the doctors did, performing what was known at the time as a standard radical mastectomy. The doctors removed her right breast, the underlying pectoral muscles under the arm (leaving her one muscle with which to operate her arm), and the lymph glands beneath the right arm. In the press conference that followed the surgery, a tired Fouty said, "I don't think that one can make the statement that she has been relieved of all malignancy. We removed all gross tumor. There was no evidence of any remaining tumor." But traces of cancer had been found in two of the thirty lymph nodes removed in the mastectomy. It would be several days before they would know if the cancer had spread.[18]

Among other unfinished business from the Nixon Administration, Gerald Ford had inherited the post-Vietnam recession. Unemployment was rising, inflation had hit double digits, and interest rates were at levels unmatched since the Civil War. To address these issues, Ford had scheduled a two-day economic summit for that

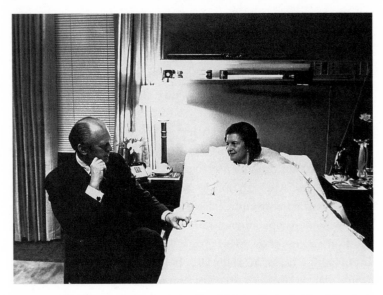

Figure 3.1. President and Mrs. Ford, Presidential Suite, Bethesda Naval Hospital, October 2, 1974 (courtesy of the Gerald R. Ford Library).

Friday and Saturday, September 26 and 27. He was to personally address the summit on its final day. His wife's operation changed everything. That Friday evening, with her mother in Bethesda awaiting surgery, Susan (who coincidentally had learned of her mother's condition from Lukash before her parents had even been told) pinch-hit for the first lady, standing by her father's side as hostess of a reception for summit delegates. The next morning, when he received the call from Lukash telling him that the lump was indeed malignant and the surgeons were removing the breast, Ford was overcome with emotion. In the Oval Office, with Hartmann working on his speech, he retreated into an adjacent bathroom; when he came out, Hartmann urged him to cry. Ford later remembered "all my tensions and fears poured out in a brief flood of tears." Ford then rushed to Bethesda. As he flew there in *Air One,* the president and his son Mike knelt in the aisle of the helicopter and prayed together. By the time they arrived, Betty was out of surgery and in the recovery room. Betty remembered that when she came out of the anesthesia and saw the long faces of her family, she moaned, "If you can't look happy, please go away. I can't bear to look at you."[19]

That afternoon, at the Washington Hilton, Ford delivered his speech to the economic summit as scheduled. At its end, he asked his audience to allow him to make "just one personal note, if I might." With his voice breaking, he informed the delegates that his wife was well, told them that "Betty would want me to be here," and earned a standing ovation from the delegates. Ford then went back to work. He later remembered that "Betty's convalescence went well, and even before her return from the hospital, I was able to devote full attention to the economy again."[20]

Had Betty Ford not opened her mouth about breast cancer after her operation, the impact of her case would still have been significant. During her hospitalization, some 45,000 letters and cards poured into the White House. Of these, perhaps the most heart-wrenching was the incredible number of letters that came from women who had had cancer or a mastectomy. They now had a role model who was in the public eye, and they simply wanted to tell Betty Ford their story. Just as important was the incredible impact that the first lady's operation had on public awareness about the disease. As early as September 27, 1975, NBC aired a report that claimed that since her surgery, six times as many women were now seeking breast screenings. In that story, reporter Betty Rollin, who herself would later be diagnosed with breast cancer, commented on how the "fear was productive" because so many women were going for mammograms: "The terror that women feel about breast cancer is not unreasonable. What is unreasonable is that women still turn their terror inward. They think if they avoid investigating the possibility that they have the disease, they'll avoid the disease. But as cases of such prominent women as Betty Ford become known, other women are turning their fear into the kind of action that can save lives."[21]

But Betty Ford was not silent about her disease. It would have been understandable if the recovery time from such an operation, particularly when joined with the other incurable diseases that were consuming her, acted to mute the desire she had shown during the vice presidency to speak out on issues of importance to her. But the experience of September 1974 would bring an epiphany to the first lady. Reporter Mary McGrory sagely observed that "what makes Mrs. Ford's [breast cancer operation] experience so poignant is that it struck her when she was beginning to flower a little." Now, she would not retreat; rather, she would now take to the stage in a way that transcended her small steps in that direction during the vice presidency. Betty Ford, congressional wife, was, for the moment at least, a thing of the past. Now, Betty Ford, the performer, would reappear. She had not only faced with dignity the possibility of her own death, she would now turn it into an opportunity to educate the nation.[22]

There was clearly room for education. In a videotape made for the Gerald R. Ford Museum, Susan Ford observed that in 1974, breast cancer surgery was "in the dark ages," and when you woke up, the patient "either had a Band-Aid, or no breast." There is much in the literature to suggest that this was true. A 1970 article showed that American medicine was woefully behind the times in terms of understanding radiation treatment, and too many mastectomies were probably being performed as a result. What was then called xeroradiography, and would later become known as mammograms, were not introduced until 1971. And yet a 1973 Gallup poll revealed that less than 20 percent of women performed regular breast self-examinations, and about half visited their physicians annually. Along with this lack of concern was what one observer called the "bosom-oriented culture" that made it socially unacceptable to have a mastectomy. Nevertheless, the disease was the leading killer of women aged forty to forty-four; in 1974, 90,000 cases of breast cancer were reported, and it would claim nearly 33,000 lives. The *New York Times* reported that in North America and Western Europe, one woman in twenty-five would die from breast cancer. Betty Ford would not be one of these victims; she went back for yearly checkups, and in November 1976 was declared cancer-free.[23]

Other celebrities had spoken out on their battles with breast cancer. In 1972, Shirley Temple Black held a bedside press conference to tell the story of her emergency mastectomy. Then only forty-four years old, the former child movie star was swamped with over 50,000 letters of concern. But her surgery occurred in the midst of the 1972 presidential election and thus did not receive the press that it might have. Also, Temple Black elected not to use her celebrity as a bully pulpit for educating women about the disease after her convalescence.[24] Also, in 1972, Senator Birch Bayh had ended his run for the presidency because his wife, Marvella, had had a mastectomy. However, short of a few interviews, Marvella Bayh, as had Temple Black, refused to become a public advocate for the issue.[25]

Betty Ford would become that advocate. It is true enough, as Mrs. Ford noted in the first volume of her memoirs, that "if I hadn't been the wife of the President of the United States, the press would not have come racing after my story." However, like Temple Black and Bayh, Mrs. Ford could have chosen to recover in private and refuse to speak to either press or public about the incident. This she did not do, for several reasons. First was her sincere belief that the time had come to speak out on the issue. A second, related reason was political in nature. The White House, still reeling from the unexpectedly harsh criticism thrown at it regarding the pardon, was now facing a press that was furious over the fact that the first lady's diagnosis and impending surgery had been kept from them for almost twenty-four hours (they did not learn of the surgery until a briefing from White House press secretary Ron Nessen, held at 7:30 PM on Friday, September 27, and their reporting from the hospital was limited to pool reports). There was concern that any stifling of news about the operation would smack of the stonewalling of Nixon's press office during Watergate. In this light, Nessen remembered that the West Wing "made the decision to be extraordinarily candid and complete in reporting on her operation and its aftermath"—a decision with which Mrs. Ford completely agreed. As she told an interviewer, "there had been so much cover-up during Watergate that we wanted to be sure there would be no cover-up in the Ford administration. So rather than continue this traditional silence about breast cancer, we felt we had to be very public."[26]

For months after the operation, the first lady—and then Happy Rockefeller, wife of the vice president, who underwent her own mastectomy and credited Mrs. Ford with making her aware of the need for self-examination—were lauded for their courage and candor as they publicly called for an increased awareness on the part of women for regular breast self-examination. Yet some have criticized Mrs. Ford for not being public enough. True, she made very few speeches that dealt with the issue. Critics like Myra Gutin, who suggested that "Mrs. Ford might have done more than give speeches to raise the country's consciousness about cancer, but chose not to," miss the point. She was the first person who held the role of first lady to so speak out on an issue of public health. In the pages of *McCall's*, this first lady was not advocating for her favorite cookie recipe; rather, she was giving instructions on how to perform breast self-exams. Her November 7, 1975 speech in New York City accepting a special award from the American Cancer Society had the most candid remarks that a first lady had ever made in public about her health:

> It isn't vanity to worry about disfigurement. It is an honest concern. I started wearing low cut dresses as soon as the scar healed, and my worries about my appearance are now just the normal ones of staying slim and keeping my hair kempt and my make-up in order. When I asked myself whether I would rather lose a right arm or a breast, I decided I would rather have lost a breast.[27]

Betty Ford was not correct when she told a historian "no one had talked about mastectomy publicly before." But she was certainly correct when she claimed that since she had been speaking out, "it's never gone underground again, which is great. I've never regretted it." In one of her final ceremonial appearances as first lady, in December 1976, she received a Communicator of Hope award from the American Cancer Society.[28]

Immediately after her hospitalization, the first lady made two changes to her staff that had been planned since the beginning of the administration. Lucy Winchester was replaced as social secretary by Nancy Lammerding, and Sheila Weidenfeld replaced Helen Smith as press secretary to the first lady. Weidenfeld's appointment would become the most important staffing decision during Betty Ford's tenure as first lady. In December 1974, Weidenfeld wrote to her boss that the proper view of the relationship between the press offices of the president and the first lady was that of master and servant: "while the West Wing sets the pace, the East Wing should always be in step." If Weidenfeld ever believed this, she did not practice it. Jack Ford would later observe that Weidenfeld "deserves a tremendous amount of credit for creating the right environment where mother could be understood and appreciated." That may well be, but from the opening gun, she crossed swords with her counterpart in the West Wing, Ron Nessen. Nessen had replaced Jerald ter-Horst, who had resigned in protest over Ford's pardon of Nixon. Taking a page from the Nixon White House, Ford's postpardon press operation—in both wings of the White House—now emphasized catering to the broadcast journalist over the print journalist. In this regard, both Weidenfeld and Nessen had strong credentials—both had worked for NBC News, Nessen as a reporter, and Weidenfeld as a producer.[29]

But neither aide followed the age-old maxim of White House staffers to toil in anonymity. Both were tremendously interested in protecting their turf, and both fought their battles noisily, and in the press. For her part, Weidenfeld wanted to expand the scope of the East Wing press operation, but she advocated her cause in a manner that made her look petty and petulant. Although her request for a wire ticker in her office was a reasonable one that had been too long unfulfilled, her requests for more government cars, more tray service from the White House mess for her staff, and other requests for White House perks were less defensible and caused needless friction. For its part, Nessen's office was often obstructionist—it took three months to get Weidenfeld her ticker—and condescending to a fault. Indeed, when it came to working with the first lady's staff, this was an attitude that pervaded the entire West Wing. Referring in a memo to two of Ford's advance men, Staff Secretary David Hoopes neatly summarized the view of the first lady's press operation as held by her husband's staff: "While on the road, [William] Greener and [John] Hushen [both deputy press secretaries] perform the functions of moving the press and seeing to their needs, and it is this role that Weidenfeld should play.... Weidenfeld should understand that her counterparts are Greener and Hushen, not Nessen, regardless of their title similarity."[30]

The battle would drone on, as most turf battles do, for the life of the administration, with no clear-cut winner, but with a loss of collegiality and effective staff work. Moreover, these feuding press operations would need to be on their toes more than ever. The first lady was about to attempt a role that only Eleanor Roosevelt and Lady Bird Johnson had attempted—Betty Ford, newly reenergized after her bout with cancer, was going to become a public lobbyist.

* * *

The revolution that scholars have called the first wave of feminism in the United States began in the mid-nineteenth century and blossomed into a fight to secure the federal suffrage for women by constitutional amendment. At the turn of the twentieth century, the National American Women's Suffrage Association (NAWSA) had won several key campaigns that gave the vote to women on the state level, but by 1910 their efforts to gain the vote for women on the federal level, largely by lobbying legislators, were at a standstill. Frustrated, Dr. Alice Paul inserted civil disobedience into the battle. A Quaker social worker who had seen firsthand the success of direct action in the drive for women's suffrage in Great Britain, Paul broke from NAWSA and in 1916 formed the National Women's Party. Members of the NWP picketed Woodrow Wilson's White House (placards read, "Mr. President, how long must women wait for liberty?"), leading to the high-profile arrest of several of the protesters. Many observers believe that without Paul's direct action, the more moderate tactics of the NAWSA would not have succeeded.[31]

After the passage of the Nineteenth Amendment in 1919, Paul turned her sights toward securing an equality for women that she felt the Constitution—despite the promises of the Fourteenth Amendment, and despite the suffrage granted by the Nineteenth Amendment—had failed to provide. In 1923, speaking in Seneca Falls, New York, as part of the seventy-fifth anniversary of the Women's Rights Convention of 1848, Paul announced what she called the "Lucretia Mott Amendment"—named for the abolitionist leader who, along with Elizabeth Cady Stanton, had organized the original Seneca Falls Convention. The original wording of what became known as the Equal Rights Amendment (ERA) is: "Men and women shall have equal rights throughout the United States and every place subject to its jurisdiction. Congress shall have the power to enforce this article by appropriate legislation."[32]

Paul hoped that an ERA would serve two purposes—to replace the huge number of state and local laws that restricted women, and to jump-start a faltering women's movement that, after it had gained the suffrage, had failed to utilize the vote in 1920 in any significant way. However, the ERA was hardly a unifying issue for feminists. Instead, it split the women's movement into two warring camps. One, led by Paul, believed that there should be complete equality of opportunity for women, with no patronizing government interference. However, another faction, led by socialist Florence Kelley and supported by notables such as Settlement House reformer Jane Addams, believed that it was the responsibility of the government to pass protective legislation (such as work-hour restrictions and child labor laws) designed to protect both women and children in society. Calling the ERA "topsy-turvy feminism," Kelley contended that "women cannot achieve true equality with men by securing identity of treatment under the law."[33]

The ERA, first introduced in Congress on December 10, 1923, would be introduced in every subsequent session of Congress up to the present day. The first significant step toward passage came in 1940, when, thanks largely to issues brought into sharper focus by the impending war—women in the military; calls for freedom elsewhere in the world (one supporter: "surely we will not refuse to our own that which we purchase for strangers with the blood of our sons")—and hoping to drive a wedge between the immensely popular Franklin D. Roosevelt and two of his most loyal groups of supporters (women and labor unions), the Republican Party endorsed the ERA in their platform. The closeness of the 1940 election, where Republican moderate Wendell Willkie ran a spirited campaign against Roosevelt, as well as the exacerbation of the above issues after Pearl Harbor, may well have led the Democratic leadership to follow suit. Four years later, despite an expected opposition from labor, the Democrats added their support in their party platform. Yet this support was more symbolic than real. Roosevelt never spoke publicly on the issue. Harry Truman supported the ERA while a senator from Missouri, but gave it a much cooler support as president. (His appointment sheet for September 21, 1945 reads in part: "12:15: Group of women sponsoring Equal Rights Amendment . . . A lot of hooey about equal rights.") Dwight Eisenhower consistently opposed the amendment. (In 1954, an adviser suggested that Ike support the ERA; his response: "Where are they unequal?") As a result of this executive ennui, along with the fact that the NWP lobby was at this point miniscule, in 1946 the Senate passed the ERA with a vote of 38–35, but it did not gain the necessary two-thirds vote to move forward. In both 1950 and 1953, the Senate passed the amendment with the necessary two-thirds vote (albeit with a rider that excepted any legislation that assisted women from the provisions of the amendment—thus, in effect, invalidating it), but in both years, the House of Representatives recessed without a vote on the issue.[34]

There were, of course, many reasons for the logjam that stalled the ERA. But the lack of an energetic women's movement behind the issue has to top the list. For many observers, this vapidity in the feminist movement had existed since 1923; after winning the suffrage, the movement was hampered, in the words of scholar Sara Evans, by the feeling that "women's battles . . . had been won." What support there was among feminists for the ERA was quickly diluted by the demands made on women to help the family survive both the Depression and World War II. There was little time for theoretical arguments. The postwar period brought with it the desire on the part of the vast majority of Americans to avoid divisive social arguments and settle into a lifestyle that reinstated the comfort and optimism of pre-Depression/prewar America. This led to a milieu where, as Evans has noted, by the 1950s, feminism was "virtually invisible."[35]

The 1960s, however, saw a fissure develop between the comfort of suburban life and the revolutionary societal issues that were pushing their way to the fore. This fissure created a climate of change that reinvigorated the women's movement. What would be termed the second wave of feminist advocacy was both caused and driven by the experiences of two groups of women. The first were professional women who were involved in the various commissions on the status of women. Activist women worked diligently on a 1961 White House Commission that began to document the problem of classification by sex. Nevertheless, the commission concluded that "a constitutional amendment need not now be sought in order to establish" the principle of equality for the sexes.[36]

The second group—younger, and of a more activist bent—had been a part of the civil rights movement and the movement against the war in Vietnam. First known as "Radical Women," and then, not altogether accurately, as the women's liberation movement, these activists placed a woman's private life—their sense, in the words of Evans, of an "invalidated life"—at the center of their concern. The 1969 Redstocking Manifesto clearly states the platform of the radicals: "We are exploited as sex objects, breeders, domestic servants, and cheap labor. . . . We do not need to change ourselves, but to change men. . . . We take the women's side in everything." As a result, the radical feminists became, in the words of Sara Evans, the "shock troops" of the abortion movement. Shulamith Firestone's 1970 treatise *The Dialectic of Sex: The Case for Feminist Revolution* was specific to this point, as she called for "the freeing of women from the tyranny of their reproductive biology by every means available, and the diffusion of the childbearing and childrearing role to the society as a whole, men as well as women."[37]

There was never a simple dichotomy to second wave feminism. These two demands—equality and liberation—grew simultaneously, and they fed each other with an intellectual vitality that caught even its participants by surprise. By the mid-1960s, feminism was also growing exponentially as society itself became more fractionalized and the left in general became more vocal and radicalized. Facing the political repercussions of a societal discord that had not been seen since the Civil War, it is not surprising that, as Evans has noted, "the U.S. Congress seemed hell-bent on figuring out just what women wanted and giving it to them." The Equal Pay Act of 1963 and the Civil Rights Act of 1964, whose Title VII prohibited job discrimination on the basis of sex, cheered all feminists. By decade's end, the time was ripe to revisit the ERA.[38]

In February 1970, twenty feminist leaders disrupted hearings of the Senate Subcommittee on Constitutional Amendments, chaired by Birch Bayh (D-IN), demanding that the ERA be taken to the floor of the Congress. On May 5, 1970, Bayh's committee began hearings on ERA. Blocked in the House by Emanuel Celler (D-NY), who had for years kept the amendment holed up in the House Judiciary Committee, Representative Martha Griffiths (D-MI) filed a discharge petition (obtaining 218 signatures) to get the ERA out of committee. Once on the floor of the House, it passed on August 10 by a vote of 352–15, with only one hour of debate.[39]

In the Senate, the main opponent of the ERA was Samuel Ervin (D-NC), who had opposed every piece of civil rights legislation that came before him as a senator. He argued that it would end all the "rational" distinctions between the two sexes based on their "physiological and functional differences" and contended that "any country that ignores these . . . differences is woefully lacking in rationality."

Bayh countered with the observation that "mothers also happen to be citizens"; Ervin summed up the anti-ERA feelings with his pithy remark, "I believe in doing something special for mothers." He tried to stop the passage of ERA by attaching a series of nine amendments. All were defeated in floor votes. On March 22, 1972, the Senate voted 84–8 to send the ERA to the states for ratification. A seven-year time limit was placed on the process. The deadline for passage was set for March 22, 1979.[40]

Early on, the proratification forces won several significant victories. Hawaii ratified the amendment on March 22, 1972, only hours after the Senate sent it to the states. The next day, Delaware, Nebraska, and New Hampshire ratified; on the third day, Idaho and Iowa followed suit. Later that year, both parties reiterated their support for the amendment by calling for its ratification in their election-year platforms. By the end of the year, twenty-two of the necessary thirty-eight states had ratified the amendment; eight more states ratified in 1973.[41]

However, by early 1973, the antiratificationists had found their sea legs. The main reason for this was the influence of Phyllis Schlafly. Born in 1924 in St. Louis, Schlafly was a Phi Beta Kappa graduate of Washington University who also held a master's degree in political science from Harvard University. She had worked as a researcher for several congressmen in Washington and had run her own unsuccessful campaign for Congress in 1952. Her 1964 book, *A Choice, Not An Echo,* endorsed the presidential campaign of Barry Goldwater and decried the hold the eastern establishment had on the Republican Party. The book turned Schlafly into one of the leading lights in the conservative movement, and in 1967, she began the publication of a monthly newsletter, the *Phyllis Schlafly Report,* a newsletter that in 1974 had 18,000 subscribers and that continues to be published to the present day. In 1970, she ran again for Congress, once again unsuccessfully.[42]

It was, however, her fight against the ERA that made Schlafly a household name. Once the fight for passage of the amendment was lost, Schlafly's "STOP-ERA" Movement took the offensive against ratification and never gave ground. On an intellectual level, the argument of the antiratificationists was that women held a privileged status under the law, and the ERA would destroy that status. They specifically exploited the widespread belief that if ERA passed, women would be drafted. In the words of the cochairmen of Florida's Citizens Against Women's Draft, "the United States would be the only country outside of the Communist bloc to allow the women of their country to be used in this fashion." But Schlafly infused this argument with rhetoric like a poke of a sharp stick. She called the supporters of ratification "liberationists . . . a bunch of bitter women seeking a constitutional cure for their personal problems." Referring to photos of an ERA rally, Schlafly sniffed: "see for yourself the unkempt, the lesbians, the radicals, the socialists." She also positioned herself as the epitome of the professional woman who proved that there was no need for the ERA: "I think I am a good example of how women can do whatever they want with their lives. They don't need legislation to have a fun, exciting, fulfilling life." Most effectively, Schlafly linked the ERA to *Roe v. Wade*. The headline of her December 1974 *Phyllis Schlafly Report* trumpeted: "ERA Means Abortion and Population Shrinkage."[43]

Schlafly's minions invaded the states with a studied organization. By the end of 1973, the movement for ratification had stalled. That year, Nebraska had rescinded its ratification; the following year, Tennessee would rescind. In 1974, only three states joined the ranks of those ratifying the amendment. By the time Ford became president, only three more states were needed for its ratification, but the fate of the ERA was very much in doubt.[44]

Schlafly's assault on the ERA was but one battle in a larger philosophical war that had torn the Republican Party since 1960, but was now approaching white-hot proportions. Dwight D. Eisenhower's popularity, accompanied by the discomfiting disintegration of the anticommunist movement as led by Senator Joseph McCarthy of Wisconsin, sent the conservative wing of the Republican Party into hiding; their calls for a policy of retaliation against communists were left largely unheeded. Many felt that Richard Nixon, the redbaiting senator from California and Khrushchev-poking vice president, would carry the conservative banner to victory in 1960, but he was ambushed at the polls by John F. Kennedy. Angered by Kennedy's failures against communism in Latin America, and fuming in opposition to his rhetoric in favor of civil rights, the right wing of the Republican Party adopted Barry Goldwater of Arizona as their champion and made plans to oppose Kennedy in 1964.

Kennedy's assassination did nothing to placate the right. Indeed, they saw Lyndon Johnson as only a little bit less evil than Kennedy. Riding a groundswell of revulsion against the federal spending of the Great Society movement, as well as a latent belief that America had gone soft on communism, Goldwater was swept to the Republican nomination, easily defeating the moderate governor of New York, Nelson Rockefeller. Goldwater's victory was largely a result of a solid organization of young conservatives—including Phyllis Schlafly, whose *A Choice, Not An Echo* served as a moderately important campaign document for the Arizonan. As Goldwater sounded the three-part conservative harmony of anticommunism, state's rights, and ultrapatriotism, the presidential campaign of 1964 effectively ignored women's issues; and although Goldwater was on record as being opposed to the ERA, it was rarely mentioned on the hustings.

Thrown into the political wilderness by Goldwater's landslide defeat at the hands of Johnson, and now forced to endure what they considered to be a half-hearted effort to win the war in Vietnam, conservatives fumed. In 1968, they found themselves putting half-hearted faith in Richard Nixon. (Although many conservatives were privately enamored of Alabama Governor George Wallace, his blatant racism made him too controversial to handle.) But even with Nixon's election they would be disappointed, as he sputtered the Vietnam War toward a five-year dénouement, and opened a détente with the Soviet Union and China that sent conservatives into fits of apoplexy. Unwilling (and unable) to challenge the Nixon juggernaut in 1972, conservatives lay in wait for the 1976 campaign.

During the hiatus of the Johnson-Nixon years, conservatives had adopted a new agenda. Issues of anticommunism were now less pressing than were social issues—affirmative action, abortion, school prayer—and the ERA. Dubbed the New Right, the champion of these new social conservatives was California Governor Ronald Reagan. Reagan's message, honed during years of practice, was deceptively simple: America had to return to values that had been sent reeling by the upheavals of the 1960s. Ideals such as family, church, and country, which Reagan perceived to have been the cornerstone of his upbringing in the nation's heartland, formed the core of his stump speeches. In this light, Ronald Reagan did not downplay his position on women's issues; indeed, for Reagan, the defeat of the ERA—a stand he took consistently in public—was a fundamental step in the direction of his desire to return to a more simple time and to restore the primacy of what he called the "traditional family."[45]

Like Truman before him, Nixon had worked for the ERA while in Congress but then largely abandoned this support as president in an effort to curry the favor of the rising New Right. But Watergate put into the White House a man who, while clearly a fiscal conservative, was a social moderate. In 1970, Gerald Ford had been instrumental in aiding Congresswoman Griffiths in obtaining the necessary number of signatures for her discharge petition for the ERA; he then voted for the amendment again, as he had done in the 1950s. As president, he continued to be both consistent and public in his support of the ERA. For example, at one occasion in 1975, Ford declared that he "wholeheartedly" endorsed the ERA, and urged that its passage be a "critical" project. However, given the growing strength of the New Right in opposition to other measures of his administration—most notably his refusal to reverse Nixon's policy of détente—Ford refused to campaign for the ERA as it made its way through the states. He never met with any group that was either for or against the issue; he did not lobby state legislators; and there is no record of his asking any member of his or the Republican National Convention staff to do so. Rather, Ford confined himself to reminding the public that "I voted for it in the House of Representatives. I can't do more than that." This president actually supported ERA. But the fight to *ratify* ERA would be taken to the public not by the president, but by the first lady.[46]

To Betty Ford—the former professional dancer and professional retailer who had, like many women in the 1950s, renounced her career and accepted the role of suburban homemaker—feminism was always an issue of choice. This view held both homemaker and career in equal esteem—as long as the woman had, in Betty's words, "the right to choose what you want to do" without being dictated to by a man. As she would write in the first volume of her memoirs, "Maybe

I ought to explain that my views on women's rights don't extend to believing that all women need to work outside the home. A housewife deserves to be honored as much as a woman who earns a living in the marketplace." Indeed, to her son Jack, her role as mother "ranked above other sympathies." Perhaps. But she consistently emphasized the right of a woman to choose her own path: "Women need to be able to make choices. That's how I see the woman's movement—as a force encouraging you to do what you want with your life. Be a wife and mother, have a home or a career, even both."[47]

For Betty, this view underwrote her entire philosophy of feminism. In a form letter sent to thousands of inquiries from citizens who wanted to know why she supported the ERA, Betty replied, "Women as homemakers and workers have been prevented from full use of their talents and management of their lives. Prevailing attitudes seriously undervalue the contributions of women as wives and mothers. One of the most important results of ratification of ERA would be to *give women more options* and to increase understanding of the choice of being homemaker and mother." It was this belief that led Mrs. Ford to make the leap from private supporter of the ERA to its most visible public lobbyist.[48]

In October 1974, Sheila Weidenfeld had dinner at the home of Liz Carpenter, former press secretary to Lady Bird Johnson, hoping to gain some insight into the pitfalls inherent in her new job. Weidenfeld's notes record a suggestion that Carpenter gave to her: "Go to five states where ERA not passed. If you can't go, get on phone and call governors. Address joint legislature in one state; 'I hope you'll pass it.'" In effect, Carpenter was asking Betty Ford to pick up the banner of political activism that had been carried by Lady Bird in her active lobbying for the 1965 Highway Beautification Act, and that had been shelved by Pat Nixon in favor of a more traditional role for the first lady. The first lady had long been on record as a supporter of the ERA, so Carpenter was preaching to the choir. However, October 1974 was simply too soon after her cancer operation for the first lady to even consider strenuous work of any kind. But by the new year, she had recuperated, and, largely as a result of her cancer scare, she had begun to reassess her role as first lady. She was now ready to make the leap from advocate to lobbyist.[49]

On January 31, 1975, political consultants Douglas Bailey and John Deardorff, whom the National Organization of Business and Professional Women had hired to work for the passage of the ERA, visited Weidenfeld. Strong supporters of the moderate Republican agenda, the two men would run Ford's advertising campaign in the 1976 election. Illinois, a state with a sizable feminist base of support, was the next state on the docket in 1975, but, as was the case in most of the midwestern states, Republican conservatives had the amendment locked in committee. The two men were fishing to see if the first lady could be induced to actively lobby Illinois legislators for the amendment. If she agreed, they felt her influence would help correct what they considered to be a misconception that was impeding ratification—that the *entire* Republican party was against its passage. Weidenfeld remembered that she wrote a memo to her boss at once, recommending that she undertake the assignment.[50]

The first lady immediately began to pen letters to the legislators. Common to each was phraseology that was hardly vague in its intent: "I support the Equal Rights Amendment because I feel that barriers to one person's freedoms in this country are impediments for all. . . . This is the year to unite against scare tactics which cloud the issues and threaten to block our chance for real equality in this country." Yet two days later, Bailey called Weidenfeld, complaining that the letters were not enough. The Illinois vote was only two days away, and Bailey pleaded for Mrs. Ford to take a more personal approach. On February 3, the first lady made what was the first of her phone calls in favor of the ERA to an Illinois legislator. The following day, the amendment cleared the committee of the Illinois legislature by a vote of 9–8. This led to more requests for phone calls, not all from professional political operatives. On February 7, Weidenfeld received a letter from a representative of Illinois's Thirty-seventh District ERA Committee, who listed their office at the campus radio station of Northern Illinois University in DeKalb. In it, the names and contact numbers of three anti-ERA legislators were given, with the plea: "Mrs. Ford's efforts on behalf of ERA have made headlines in Illinois, and any help she could give us would be appreciated greatly."[51]

According to Mrs. Ford, the tone of her calls was a decided "soft sell. . . . I merely asked that the amendment be allowed to get to the floor and to let people vote their conscience."[52] The only transcripts

Figure 3.2. Mrs. Ford in the Queen's Bedroom, White House living quarters, February, 1975 (courtesy of the Gerald R. Ford Library).

of those calls exist in Weidenfeld's memoirs, but they tend to corroborate Mrs. Ford's own assessment of her technique. Witness a call to a Missouri legislator:

> Hello . . . How are you Mrs. Miller? Now, don't be bowled over, we have to keep you on your feet! . . . Well, it's a pleasure talking to you . . . I realize you're under a lot of pressure with the voters today, but I'm just calling to let you know that the President and I are considerably interested. . . . Yes, we are both interested in the outcome. . . . I think the ERA is so important . . . I think you have to vote your conscience.[53]

Throughout the first weeks of February, Mrs. Ford continued to work the phones, often wearing the neck brace she used to help flare-ups from her pinched nerve. She called legislators in North Dakota, Illinois, Nevada, Missouri, North Carolina, Indiana, Montana, Oklahoma, and Arizona. But this was not the extent of her involvement. She also called a meeting of White House staffers who, on their lunch hour, came to hear a talk from Bailey and Deardorff regarding the importance of passing the amendment. Weidenfeld noted, "Mrs. Ford seems to love it" (Figure 3.2).[54]

As important as the lobbying itself, however, was the fact that it ultimately had no appreciable impact on the issue. Perhaps one reason was a backlash against her calls from legislators who may, before being contacted by the first lady, have been sitting on the fence. Indeed, many legislators rebelled against the tactic. Illinois legislator Donald Deuster angrily wrote Mrs. Ford, arguing that she had no right to interfere in the legislative process and requesting that she "immediately desist in your long-distance telephone lobbying campaign and that you refrain from using the prestige of the White House and your position of First Lady . . . to promote adoption of this . . . amendment." Illinois ended up defeating the amendment, a result that Mrs. Ford labeled as "disheartening and confusing." Soon after, on April 16, 1975, North Carolina voted down the ERA, 62–57. Only one state, North Dakota, ratified the amendment in 1975. No further votes were scheduled until 1976, and being a national election year, the amendment stayed stalled.[55]

In the wake of the ERA battle, one friend said of the first lady, "After 26 years in his shadow, she's in the limelight now." In his memoirs, Gerald Ford makes no reference whatsoever to his wife's efforts on behalf of the ERA.[56]

CHAPTER 4

"I JUST FIGURED THAT IT WAS TIME THAT SOMEBODY SPOKE UP"

Almost thirteen cubic feet of mail descended on the White House regarding the first lady's lobbying for the ERA; it ran three to one against her lobbying efforts. A sampling: "What right do you have as a representative of all women to contact the legislators and put pressure on them to pass the hated ERA?" "You are no lady—first, second or last. Keep your stupid views to yourself from now on." "It is things like this silly ERA Amendment . . . that will someday see commuisium [*sic*] take over the U.S. . . . . I know my place in life as a woman and I'm equal to no man because that is how God intended." And "Our recent history has seen this nation's First Ladies dedicating themselves to restoring the White House; beautifying America; and remaining silent. You, Mrs. Ford, should take an example from this latter group." Pickets surrounded the White House—and for the first time in modern memory, they weren't picketing the president, but his wife. Signs read, "Betty Ford, Get Off the Phone." Indeed, with some pride in her voice, Mrs. Ford would often use the line, "I'm the only First Lady to ever have a march organized against her."[1]

Aside from being a public relations problem for the Ford Administration, there was a larger legal question that the first lady's lobbying brought to the fore: could such lobbying be legally undertaken from within the White House? Phyllis Schlafly argued that this presented a states' rights issue; because the Constitution left the final step in the ratification process to the states, it was unconstitutional for the federal government (and thus the first lady) to interfere in any way. After finding out that Betty had presented a slide show on the ERA to members of her staff, Schlafly wrote the White House asking for equal time, as well as "an accounting of how much federal money has been spent by you and other White House personnel in making long distance calls to legislators, and how much federal money has been spent on the salaries of federal employees working for ratification of the ERA." When a reporter asked the first lady if she would agree to a debate with Schlafly, she sniffed, "I wouldn't waste my time."[2]

By the end of the spring 1975, Ford's staff felt that it had to intervene. White House Counsel Philip Buchen wrote a rather curt note to the first lady's staff, reminding them that "if there were to be activities intended to influence the public on legislation before the Congress, my office should be consulted before any steps are taken."[3] The West Wing also attempted to script the first lady, creating a document that contained a list of proposed talking points in case she was asked about her advocacy and lobbying for the ERA:

General Points:

. . . all I'm doing is expressing my opinion . . .

. . . (on spending government money for phone calls)—You know, I'm in a strange position. My home is also a government office—and short of having a pay phone installed, I haven't figured out another way to do it. . . .

You have not spent any government money in doing this . . . (specifically, the ERA briefings were on lunch time, employees coming *voluntarily* (about 160 came), and the calls you've made have been brief—only expressing your opinion—and on a Wats line.[4]

Mrs. Ford tried to put the best face on the criticism, telling the *New York Times* that "it is those who are against [the ERA] who are doing the writing. Those who are for it sit back and say, 'Good for her—push on.'" But it was clear that the president's advisers did not wish her to push on, and ultimately, she did not. Although the first lady continued her public statements in favor of the ERA (in March 1976 she appeared at an ERAmerica-sponsored Helen Reddy concert and appeared on stage with the singer to once again voice her support for the amendment), by spring 1975, her private lobbying of legislators all but stopped. It seems clear in retrospect that pressure brought to bear against the first lady from the West Wing was largely responsible for the cooling of Betty's lobbying ardor.[5]

The first lady's lobbying was far from the only headache she created for her husband's advisers. A potential nightmare of equal proportions was the ever-present possibility that her alcohol and substance abuse could become a public issue. It had come close. As noted earlier, during a trip to Georgia as second lady, Mrs. Ford had admitted that she took a Valium per day. Sheila Weidenfeld remembered that Betty would tell essentially the same story to a *Newsweek* reporter, except that she added the detail that her psychiatrist had prescribed the medication. The comments were buried by the events of the final days of Watergate, but after Ford became president, the issue arose again. When asked by a reporter about the first lady's use of painkillers, Press Secretary Jerald terHorst referred to her pinched nerve. However, he almost gave away the store when he responded that "tranquilizers and alcohol failed to relax her suffering." This was the first public uttering of the possibility of the first lady's alcohol abuse. Some in the press suspected, yet she was never fully investigated by the press as to the degree of her drug and alcohol consumption. The closest that any reporter came to making an allegation was in a September 1975 article in *Good Housekeeping*. Responding to a question about the condition of her osteoarthritis, Betty told reporter Myra MacPherson that the pain "radiates all down my left arm, leg, and side." MacPherson then opined: "This medication had led to rumors that she is at times overly drugged. Both she and her doctors deny this."[6]

In the first volume of her memoirs, Betty claimed, "I was fine when I was in the White House." By her own later admissions, this was a falsehood. In the second volume, she was more circumspect: "truthfully, it *was* better in the White House. I flowered. Jerry was no longer away so much. And I was somebody, the First Lady." This was a claim that she would repeat through the years. Some years later, she claimed that "the demands on me filled up those spaces when I might have thought about a drink." In relative terms, during the excitement of the White House years, it is possible that the pace of her drinking did indeed slow. But one does not turn off a disease simply because one has become first lady. Betty's drinking continued through the congressional and vice presidential years, and it continued while she was in the White House. As had been the case with her immediate family, the people around Betty—even her doctors—noticed, knew, and did nothing. As Ron Nessen noted in his memoirs, "Mrs. Ford's family and friends were concerned about her dependence but kept the problem a closely guarded secret."[7] Nancy Howe was one of those friends.

Upon moving into the White House, the bond between Nancy Howe and the woman she indiscreetly referred to in public as "Petunia" had grown to mammoth proportions. Deliberately circumspect about the Howe relationship in the first volume of her memoirs, Mrs. Ford would only say that "for a time, she was a very close friend." This is an understatement. After Ford became president, the two women were inseparable. They were so close that Howe literally moved into the White House, choosing for herself a third floor bedroom and spending several nights a week there.[8]

For almost two years, Howe was the most important person on Betty Ford's staff; after the cancer operation, she became the most important person in Betty Ford's life. All access to the first lady went not through the East Wing staff, but through Howe. Indeed, the formal East Wing staff as a group never had the influence that Howe personally had over the first lady. That staff often received their daily information about the first lady's schedule—and the first lady's condition—from Howe. As a result, virtually everyone in the White House resented Howe. Part of it was petty jealousy. In January 1975, someone on the staff noticed that Howe was making more money than either Weidenfeld or Lammerding; their salaries were soon made equal. But the resentment ran deeper than just money. Most staffers, as well as members of the First Family, complained that Howe kept too tight a control over entrée to the first lady. They also resented her relentless courting of the press. On this latter score, Weidenfeld relates a story that suggests that even Betty was getting a bit tired of her friend's seeming need to be in the public eye. When an article appeared in the March 2, 1975, issue of *Family Weekly* under the title "Betty Ford's Best Friend," Weidenfeld remembered that the first lady, calling her from Camp David, was "hysterical." Mrs. Ford raged, "She is not my best friend! I am so mad right now . . . I'm going to fire Nancy!"[9]

But she didn't. Theirs was a tremendously complicated relationship, one well known in Washington life. Howe had attached herself to a powerful woman, and her instant celebrity—one that she fed through her press contacts—was solely a function of their friendship. In this regard, Weidenfeld's harshly worded assessment has more than a ring of truth: "It is clearly a case of fame by association. And that is what is so sad. Nancy was so dazzled by the glitter of celebrity politics that she mistook parasites for friends." At the same time, however, the first lady saw Howe's services and friendship to a first lady who was in the throes of several diseases and had recently faced imminent death as a result of one of them, to be irreplaceable. She even placed that friendship above the attentions of her daughter. Mrs. Ford later admitted that Howe had restricted Susan Ford's access to her mother, and she weakly apologized that "I loved Susan, but I was dependent on Nancy."[10]

But acting as Betty Ford's gatekeeper was not Howe's only role. Indeed, it may not have been her most important. According to *Washington Post* reporter Maxine Cheshire, the first lady "needed Nancy Howe virtually to get through the day," and at the end of that day, "the two would sit for a cocktail hour that was viewed with displeasure by the president." This displeasure was more than a little ironic; Howe may well have simply joined the president as one of the two chief enablers of the first lady's substance abuse. But this was masked by Mrs. Ford's genuine true need for a friend, and, perhaps to some degree, by a sense of beholdenness—after all, it was she who suggested that the first lady accompany her to the medical examination that had saved Betty Ford's life.[11]

Turf wars between a friend to those in power and others serving those in power are to be expected—and the confrontations between Howe and other White House staffers were classic. For the first eight months of the administration, they fought to a draw. Few of her colleagues liked her, but Howe had the complete support of the first lady. Then came the revelation of a scandal that, if true, could prove awkward for a Ford White House struggling to extricate itself from the ghosts of Watergate.

Maxine Cheshire had been keeping files on a garish Korean lobbyist named Tongsun Park. Park, the founder and owner of the Georgetown Club, had extensive business interests in shipping, oil and rice imports, and real estate. He had entertained some of Washington's most powerful, including House Majority Leader Thomas P. "Tip" O'Neill, former Defense Secretary Melvin Laird, and Soviet Ambassador Anatoly Dobrynin. Some sources suggested that Park's lavish lifestyle was being bankrolled by South Korean intelligence. When asked about his motives, however, Park innocently replied, "I simply like to entertain. I'm a social catalyst who likes to bring people together."[12]

On April 3, 1975, Cheshire, who in her own words had become "rather chummy" with Nancy Howe, called Weidenfeld to inform the White House that she was about to break a story regarding Howe, her husband James, and their daughter Lise Courtney, who was now working at the Federal Communications Commission. Cheshire informed Weidenfeld that she had learned that the Howes, with their daughter, were at that moment vacationing in the Dominican Republic as the guests of Park. According to Cheshire, Park himself was not with the Howes; he had delegated the duties of host to his girlfriend, Tandy Meams Dickenson, and Dickenson paid the Howes' $1,475 hotel bill. Also, Cheshire had learned that Park had invited the Howes to join him in Mexico the previous Christmas at his own expense. According to Cheshire, Lise Courtney accepted Park's invitation and flew to Mexico while her parents cashed in their tickets, stayed home, and kept the money for themselves. Weidenfeld remembered in her memoirs that she called Betty, told her what she knew, and that the first lady's reaction was a muted, "Park entertains everyone."[13]

The next day, Weidenfeld called Howe, who angrily denied all the allegations and said that she would call Cheshire directly. Cheshire remembered going to Howe's home to confront her with her facts. According to Cheshire, James Howe confirmed much of her story, then turned to his wife: "There, I've destroyed you. You don't have a White House job any more. You can stay home. Or you can get a job as a tour guide in the Dominican Republic." According to a later published report, after their meeting, James Howe reneged, calling Cheshire several times to say that his wife had repaid Mrs. Dickenson, calling her "absolutely innocent," and begging that the story be killed because its publication would embarrass his family and possibly lead to a divorce. On April 8, Rumsfeld called Weidenfeld to ask about the story and to report that *Washington Post* publisher Ben Bradlee, at the request of Nancy and James Howe's psychiatrist—who was labeling Nancy as unstable—had shelved the story, at least for the time being. Some time during that period, White House counsel Philip Buchen began an investigation into the matter and spoke for the first time to James and Lise Courtney Howe to try to establish the facts of the story.[14]

On April 10, James Howe shot and killed himself. The next day, the *Washington Post* ran not only the story of Howe's suicide, but also Cheshire's story of the relationship between the Howes and Tongsun Park. Cheshire's story also revealed that Howe had been being treated at Walter Reed Hospital on a "continuing basis" for alcoholism (over the past two years, he had had two alcohol-related automobile accidents, and his driver's license had been suspended), and that both he and his wife had been seeing a psychiatrist—the same psychiatrist who had only days before called Bradlee to ask him to drop the story on the investigation of Howe. Of the story, Bradlee reportedly growled, "this is the most fucking unreal thing that has ever happened at this newspaper."[15]

Weidenfeld remembered that Mrs. Ford, who along with Susan attended Howe's funeral on April 13, exclaimed to her, "Maxine Cheshire killed Jimmy Howe!" But almost instantly, James Howe ceased to be the story. It was duly reported that he had repaid Park for the Dominican Republic trip, from which both he and his wife had profited, but the story of the cashed-in tickets from the Mexico trip looked like it would have legs. The obligatory White House investigation into the gift tickets began immediately, and a decision was made with astounding—some said cold-hearted—speed. On April 16, less than a week after the suicide of her husband, the White House announced that Nancy Howe would be leaving the employ of Betty Ford after she completed a six-week leave of absence. When asked whether the actions of the White House had been callous, Howe snapped, "You said it, I didn't. I just don't want to talk about it."[16]

But Mrs. Ford did not want Howe to be fired. She wanted to keep her friend nearby, and, in her words, "be with [her] through that period." The day after James Howe's suicide, the first lady snapped to a reporter that there was "no question" that Nancy Howe would continue as her personal assistant, and that "she will return as soon as she feels up to it." But, as she later bemoaned, she "wasn't permitted" to do so. The White House had decided that Nancy Howe must go.[17]

Thus, the reason that has been offered by Mrs. Ford and accepted by most of the principals for Howe's firing—that Howe's "own psychologists and another psychologist met with Dr. Lukash and decided that she wasn't in shape to stay on"—is highly suspect. In the post-Watergate milieu, the press was about to initiate another scandal-driven feeding frenzy. Ford's own White House had written a code of ethics that forbade White House employees from accepting gifts of any kind from anyone "who has or is seeking contractual or business dealings with any department or agency in the executive branch or who has any interests which may be substantially affected by the performance of your job." Given the fact that the Howe family's relationship with Park certainly seemed, on the surface at least, to violate this code, the fact that Nancy Howe was ultimately sacrificed is not surprising. Yet there was more to Howe's removal than just the code of ethics. Indeed, as reporter Sarah McClendon pointed out at a news briefing on April 11, other members of the administration had been accused of violating the code for actions such as accepting free airline tickets, and had not been "pulled off from work . . . and . . . investigated" (Nessen simply ignored McClendon's comment). One other reason for her removal should be offered: Gerald Ford may well have wanted it that way, scandal or no scandal. As Cheshire later put it, Ford was "aware of his wife's drinking. He was determined to put a stop to it, and his plan was to split up the drinking buddies."[18]

Buchen, whose files show that he was the administration point man for the investigation of both James and Nancy Howe, was the trigger man. Ford's close friend and Grand Rapids law partner would write to another friend that "the situation and its outcome proved tremendously disturbing to me, but I knew of no better way of handling the problem." The dismissal of Howe gained for the White House precisely the reaction it had hoped. A memo to

Buchen suggests that Tom Kendrick of the *Washington Post* called after Howe's resignation and said that the *Post* was going to "low-key" the story of the link between the Howes and Park—which is what happened.[19]

The first lady's staff difficulties did not end with the dismissal of Nancy Howe. Recently married Social Secretary Nancy Lammerding Ruwe had often displayed a brusque style that clashed with Rumsfeld's equally prickly demeanor. In August 1975, she left the administration. Weidenfeld's handwritten notes offer one scenario: "Mrs. F[ord] said she had lunch with Nancy. They discussed Nancy's wanting to resign because of new house, marriage. . . . Mrs. F[ord] said she was disappointed because Nancy had done such an excellent job." Others gossiped that Rumsfeld had engineered her dismissal. For three months, Betty planned her own social engagements. In October, Maria Downs was hired to replace Lammerding Ruwe. Downs had a résumé filled with jobs in Republican Party politics, including stints as director of women's programs at the Republican National Committee, and special assistant to Anne Armstrong. Just as important, Downs was universally seen to be Rumsfeld's candidate for the job (she was listed in *Newsweek* as a part of "Rummy's Network"). Downs would stay on until the end of the administration.[20]

Yet to a White House staff that was clearly nervous about its very public first lady, a staff housecleaning was not enough to calm their anxieties. With the criticism of the ERA still resonating in the streets, the West Wing now moved to limit the first lady's ability to publicly advocate for issues that concerned her. On January 9, 1975, Ford signed Executive Order 11832, establishing a National Commission on the Observance of National Women's Year. At the signing ceremony, Ford reminded his audience that he "wholeheartedly" endorsed the ERA, and asked that "1975, International Women's Year, be the year that the ERA is ratified." In her response to her husband's remarks, the first lady quipped, "I just want to congratulate you, Mr. President. I am glad to see you have come a long, long way." Although there is no record of Mrs. Ford having lobbied her husband in favor of the creation of the commission, she clearly gave him a great deal of credit in her memoirs: "It had moral force; it meant a President of the United States was standing up for women and the ERA, and against 'legal inequities between sexes.'"[21]

Yet when Ford announced his Commission on the International Women's Year three months later, a commission chaired by Jill Ruckelshaus and including such notables as actors Alan Alda and Katherine Hepburn, his wife was conspicuously absent from its membership. When she was invited to travel to Mexico City and participate in the International Women's Year Conference, the State Department opposed her participation, ostensibly because of expected "anti-American speeches and resolutions" that might be introduced, as well as "concerns over the expected tenor of debate." Despite the lobbying of Ruckelshaus, Nancy Kissinger, and Leah Rabin, wife of the then Prime Minister of Israel, when it became clear that, as recalled in the notes of Sheila Weidenfeld, the "U.S. was going to get clobbered" and that there was a "chance of her being embarrassed," the first lady was not allowed to participate.[22]

Lobbying could be limited; staffers could be fired; and candor could be controlled. But as the Ford staffers—and her husband—would learn to their chagrin, Betty Ford's outspokenness could not long be muted. After all, as she later remembered, "When [my husband's] aides disapproved of what I said, I didn't let it bother me. I just figured that it was time that somebody spoke up."[23]

In early March 1975, producer Don Hewitt of CBS News contacted Weidenfeld to pitch the idea of interviewing Betty Ford on the wildly popular television news magazine program *60 Minutes*. Weidenfeld remembered in a diary entry that "I would love her to do it, because it is the best produced show on the air, one of the only programs capable of portraying people as they really are." It bears noting that such an invitation was, in and of itself, news. Nothing of the sort had come to either Lady Bird Johnson or Pat Nixon; the nearest thing was the now-famous January 1962 tour of the White House that Jacqueline Kennedy had given to Charles Collingwood, also of CBS News. Moreover, the first lady had proven herself to be outspoken enough to carry her end of a prime time interview, and more than able to make it interesting to what would be a potentially gargantuan viewing audience. An internal CBS briefing memo written before the taping of the interview gushed about the perception of Mrs. Ford as "an unusual First Lady" who had expressed her opinion, was "also a traditional woman," and whose courage was "touching and inspiring—not for sad reasons." It also admitted that like many Americans, "Betty Ford surprised us."[24]

Yet it should also be considered that Betty Ford should not have accepted the invitation to do the interview. She was unpredictable in live interviews—witness her performance in her first press conference. The Howe scandal was still fresh. (In retrospect, it is surprising that she was not asked any questions about it.) Most importantly, the interview was to be conducted by a seasoned veteran. Morley Safer, formerly a Canadian journalist, had made his name reporting in Vietnam (Safer opened the CBS network's Saigon Bureau in 1965 and was then made chief of the network's London bureau). Known for his chivalrous, nonconfrontational style, Safer was seen by the White House as a safe choice for the interview. Nevertheless, given his background, it was clear that this would not be an interview that concentrated on the color of the drapes in the East Room. Ultimately, Mrs. Ford agreed to the interview, but at the last minute, she almost backed out, suggesting to Weidenfeld that her son Jack be interviewed in her stead. Weidenfeld bucked up the first lady, and on July 21, 1975, the show was videotaped in the White House Solarium[25] (Figure 4.1).

Safer softballed the beginning of the interview, allowing her, for example, to answer questions about how she saw her role as first lady ("I told my husband if we have to go to the White House, okay, I will go, but I'm going as myself, and it's too late to change my pattern, and if they don't like it then they'll just have to throw me out"). He then asked several personal questions, none of which was wholly unexpected—such as whether she thought her husband had ever had an affair ("right now he still enjoys a pretty girl. And he really doesn't have time for outside entertainment because I keep him busy"), and if she had ever gone to a psychiatrist (admitting she had, she responded that "I was a little beaten down, and he built up my ego"). Safer also observed that any first lady lived in the shadow of the president. (Disagreeing, Mrs. Ford quipped to Safer, "You can ask me any question. I'm perfectly happy to answer and give you my idea, and I'm sure my husband won't mind at all.")

To this point in the interview, the first lady was not just calm, but seemed a master of the medium. Clearly Safer's equal on screen, her

Figure 4.1. Mrs. Ford and Morley Safer, West Sitting Hall, White House,
July 21, 1975 (courtesy of the Gerald R. Ford Library).

combination of one-liners and thoughtful answers to his questions made for compelling viewing. But Safer felt that "the interview was going nowhere. It was OK and nothing more." Thus, he shifted his line of questioning toward the first lady's relationship with her children. He eased into the topic by asking her if she felt that it was acceptable for young people to live together before they were married. Her response—"Well, they are, aren't they?"—led Safer to his next question. As he remembers it, "the question about Susan Ford just popped into my head."[26] Safer shot back: "Well, what if Susan Ford came to you and said, 'Mother, I am having an affair?'" The question clearly caught Mrs. Ford off-guard—it was the first to noticeably do so. She did a complete double-take at Safer, and responded:

> Certainly—well, I wouldn't be surprised. I think she's a perfectly normal human being, like all young girls. If she wanted to continue it, I would certainly counsel and advise her on the subject. And I'd want to know pretty much about the young man she was planning to have the affair with—whether it was a worthwhile encounter, or whether it was going to be one of those—she's pretty young to start affairs.

Safer then countered, "Old enough?" She did not back down: "She's a big girl."

Next, Safer asked her if she thought that her kids had smoked marijuana. In an almost casual way, she remarked that she believed that they had probably tried it. When asked if "Betty Bloomer would have been the kind of girl who would have at least experimented with marijuana when you were growing up," she responded "Oh, I'm sure I probably . . . I probably wouldn't have gone into it as a habit or anything like that. It's the type of thing that young people have to experience, like your first beer or your first cigarette, something like that."[27]

In many ways, the *60 Minutes* interview was but one further example of the coming of age of the broadcast media after Vietnam and Watergate. The time was also right for the media to treat the first lady as the subject of an in-depth interview. As scholar Gil Troy has noted, "Encouraged by . . . the sexual revolution reporters posed questions they would not have dared ask ten years before." Thinking back to the interview, Weidenfeld pondered, "would anyone have dared ask Mamie Eisenhower about subjects like that?" Nevertheless, it was clear that it was in the *answers* to those questions that the White House would endure a stunning amount of disparagement.[28]

The interview was broadcast on August 10, 1975—one year and one day after Gerald Ford had become president. Safer later argued that "all Betty Ford was doing was expressing moderate maternal feelings." Perhaps. She would later protest in a 1995 interview that "I was trying to be as frank as possible. I certainly wasn't going to sit there and say my children hadn't tried drugs when I know. . . ." Catching herself, she finished her thought: "well, you know what the times were like then." Following the interview, the times, at least for Mrs. Ford, were tumultuous; she was overly charitable when she noted that "my stock with the public did not go up." Son Steve was closer to the mark: "she got fried, at first." Weighing in against the first lady's comments were the Greater Houston Clergy Association, the Knights of Columbus of Pennsylvania, several mayors from southern states, many newspaper editorials, and Maria Von Trapp of Vermont. When the siege of the White House mailroom had slowed down, some 28,000 letters had inundated the White House, the majority of them critical of the first lady. Middle Americans, particularly in the heartland, were outraged.[29]

Mrs. Ford's critics concentrated on her moral stand. Not surprisingly, the far-right *Manchester Union Leader* led the way: "the immorality of Mrs. Ford's remarks is almost exceeded by their stupidity . . . a disgusting spectacle. Coming from the first lady in the White House, it disgraces the nation itself." One woman correspondent noted, "Have we not the right to expect a more genteel, lofty moral code in the woman who willingly or not represents American womanhood?" Even the usually reserved Michael Ford, then a divinity student, publicly expressed his disapproval with his mother's views on premarital sex. For her part, however, Susan Ford was defensive. At a news conference in Seabrook Island, South Carolina, she emphatically stated that she was not going to have an affair, but she saw "nothing wrong" with her mother's comments, and that she and her mother had "very, very similar ideas." Later, she laughed it off, as she observed: "Imagine a teenager having your mother support your right to have an affair. I didn't want to have an affair—but try telling that to teenage boys."[30]

Inside the White House, the blame for the interview was laid at the doorstep of Sheila Weidenfeld. Although she defiantly remembered for a reporter that "Nobody on the White House staff except me wanted the first lady to do the program," her colleagues in the West Wing told the same reporter that Weidenfeld was a "kooky, irresponsible kid," and "as a press secretary she should have her head examined." Jack Angell, a veteran Chicago newscaster, blamed Weidenfeld for the fallout from the interview, writing her that for her "to risk a sensitive interview with the likes of Morley Safer is not really profound PR judgment. He may be safer, but he ain't safe."[31]

The furor over the interview threw Ford into a defensive posture. Weidenfeld remembered that Ford turned to his wife and quipped, "you just cost me 10 million votes . . . No, you just cost me 20 million votes." Chief of Staff Donald Rumsfeld, watching with the First Family, disagreed: "Nonsense. She just won you 30 million votes." Ron Nessen, who witnessed the exchange, remembered that the president underscored his view of the situation by throwing a pillow at his wife. Ford would later remember, "I was really kidding her because I happen to feel very strongly that the American people like frankness"; his wife would later agree that her husband's reaction was "facetious." But the White House found nothing funny in the public furor that her interview had precipitated. In an internal memo, Nessen argued that "it is important that the President not take back or disavow anything Mrs. Ford said . . . I believe it is a mistake to continue to shrug off the public controversy over Mrs. Ford's remarks as harmless and without political effect." If this advice was passed on to Ford, he did not heed it. Instead, he went on the hustings and tried to explain away his wife's comments. In Milwaukee, he said, "Let me put this in proper perspective . . . What Betty was really trying to say was because of the closeness of our family and the understanding between children and parents, we are deeply concerned by the moral standards by which the family has been raised. . . . So, I am real proud of what Betty tried to say and I regret there might have been some misunderstanding of what she did say."[32]

This only exacerbated the situation. Many things can be said about the *60 Minutes* interview, but it is impossible to misunderstand what Betty Ford meant. White House observer John Osborne sighed, "It's too bad the president felt he had to apologize for his wife's candor." Kitty Dukakis, then the first lady of Massachusetts, took Ford to task for his condescending tone by saying that she "felt betrayed when I read that President Ford felt it necessary to articulate" his wife's views on premarital sex, and observed that "I feel Mrs. Ford articulated what many of us have found refreshing."[33]

Mrs. Dukakis's observations are particularly telling. The White House was only beginning to understand the depth of the anger of the New Right. Although Ford had been given a short honeymoon after he took office, the pardon of Nixon, followed close on the heels of his approval of an amnesty program for Vietnam-era deserters and protesters, galvanized conservatives into action. Waiting in the wings was Ronald Reagan, and through the latter part of 1975, he hammered at Ford's mishandling of the economy and détente, as well as his support for the ERA, which Reagan felt would destroy the American family. In such a climate, it is understandable that the Ford White House saw Betty Ford's *60 Minutes* comments as holding the possibility for ammunition for the right. Ford himself believed that the reaction to the interview was one of "several different factors [that] would come together in the summer of 1975 to make a Reagan challenge inevitable."[34]

* * *

As the administration entered the fall of 1975, fallout from both within and outside the White House over a television interview was hardly the only thing on the first lady's mind. Betty Ford also faced—not once, but twice—the specter of her husband's mortality. On September 5, 1975, Ford traveled to Sacramento, California, to meet with Governor Jerry Brown and to give a speech to the California legislature on the subject of crime. Ford was walking across the grounds of the state capitol when he paused to shake some hands. As he remembered what happened next, "I spotted a woman wearing a red dress. When I slowed down, I noticed immediately that she thrust her hand under the arms of the other spectators. I reached down to shake it—and looked into the barrel of a .45 caliber pistol pointed directly at me. I ducked." Secret Service Agent Larry Buendorf grabbed the gun. It was loaded, but there was no bullet in the chamber. The assailant, Lynette "Squeaky" Fromme, had gained notoriety as a member of the "family" of convicted mass murderer Charles Manson. In this instance, however, Fromme professed to be upset with Ford's stance on nuclear power. For her part, Mrs. Ford was back in Washington at the time of the first assassination attempt. Ford immediately phoned her and remembered later that she sounded "concerned." The first lady simply told the press that the threat of assassination was "something you have to live with."[35]

Less than a month later, on September 22, Ford once again found himself in California, this time to address the annual meeting of the AFL-CIO Building and Construction Trades Unions in San Francisco. Extra security had been arranged because of Fromme's botched attempt. Ford exited the St. Francis Hotel and paused momentarily to wave at a crowd that had formed across the street. A woman wearing sunglasses and a raincoat pulled a pistol from her handbag. This time, the gun fired. The bullet struck the wall of the hotel to Ford's right, ricocheted, struck the curb to Ford's left, and bounced up, hitting a taxi driver in the groin. The intervention of ex-marine Oliver Sipple, who hit her arm, made the shot go wild. Ford was pushed into his car, and his Secret Service agents piled on top of him.[36]

Ford later described his second assailant, Sara Jane Moore, as "a forty-five year old matron . . . who had ties to radical groups in the

San Francisco area." Moore was much more. A native of West Virginia, she had served as an informant for the FBI as well as for the Federal Bureau of Alcohol, Tobacco, and Firearms and the local police. She had been picked up on a minor weapons charge only twenty-four hours before the shooting and released. The authorities took away her pistol when they detained her, but she simply purchased another one. Moore's self-expressed motive: "I thought there would be chaos [following an assassination], and that chaos would be the catalyst for the winds of change."[37]

That day, Mrs. Ford had been visiting friends in Monterey. Upon her arrival in San Francisco, she boarded *Air Force One*. Not yet having heard about the incident, she gaily asked her husband, "Well, how did they treat you in San Francisco?" Ford was incredulous— "You mean you don't know?" The rest of their conversation was lost, as the passengers found relief from the day's events in shouted greetings and cocktails. Nessen remembered that he had "watched [Mrs. Ford's] face intently to see what her reaction would be. She never changed her expression. She just kept smiling and sipped her drink."[38]

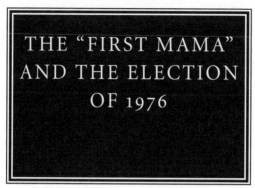

CHAPTER 5

THE "FIRST MAMA"
AND THE ELECTION
OF 1976

By fall 1975, Betty Ford was under serious fire from within the White House. Many of her husband's advisers—and, according to some evidence, her husband himself—believed that she had become a political liability. She most certainly understated the case when she told *People* magazine that "I'm sure my husband's staff says, 'Well, what are we going to do with her now?'"[1]

However, a significant portion of the public believed that Betty was actually an asset to the administration. That fall, her polls were not only the highest of any first lady to that point in history, but—in an even more significant fact—her numbers were higher than her husband's. A Harris Poll released on November 10, 1975 showed absolutely no doubt that the first lady was in synch with the majority of the nation. Sixty percent of those asked supported her statement when she said that "if her daughter were having an affair, she would want to know if the young man were nice or not"; 70 percent agreed with her stand favoring the passage of the ERA. Asked in another poll whether they felt that her opinions would hurt the president's chances, 63 percent said no. The pattern of the backing that the first lady received was noteworthy. Those most solidly behind her were people who lived on the East and West Coasts, people who lived in big cities and suburbs, people under thirty, and those who had either a liberal or an independent political philosophy. Those who did not support her were those who lived in the South, were rural residents, were aged fifty and older, and were more conservative in bent. In a nutshell, she was polling low among those constituencies who could be counted upon to vote against her husband in a Republican presidential primary and instead support conservative icon Ronald Reagan, who was about to challenge the president for the Republican nomination.[2]

An explanation for this phenomenon was that the vast majority of Americans were still in the political middle, and the Gerald R. Fords were seen as the middle personified. The national love affair with this family, established during the abbreviated vice presidency and perpetuated largely in the women's magazines, was not sullied by the controversial events of his presidency—quite the contrary. Despite their disagreements with the president on issues, and despite their disagreements with Betty over her advocacy and lobbying, America continued to love the Fords of Grand Rapids.

In mid-1975, Betty opined, "Both Jerry and I are very ordinary, humble people who enjoy life and are not impressed with ourselves." Humble, perhaps. But ordinary was in the eye of the beholder. The Ford children were certainly not ordinary when compared to previous First Broods. They were, in the words of the mater familias, "one big scrappy family," and it was clearly a family which the nation related to and enjoyed. To observe that all four children were opinionated, thoughtful, blunt, and going through a variety of growing pains did not separate them from the Nixon and Johnson girls. However, the fact that they often aired their family disagreements in the press—and refused to tone down their youthful vigor and angst to service their father's political ambitions—did.[3]

Of all the Ford children, Mike was the most determined to avoid the limelight; he even took a job under an assumed name so as to avoid the camera's glare. Twenty-four years old in 1974, he was enrolled in Cornwall Divinity School in Essex, Massachusetts, as was his wife, the former Gayle Ann Brumbaugh. (They had met while they were both at Wake Forest University.) Both were interested in working with children, perhaps in a counseling mode. Yet when he felt himself cornered by the media, Mike was direct with his answers. For example, he disagreed with his father's pardoning of

Nixon, suggesting that Nixon owed the public a "total confession" for his crimes—a statement from which the White House had to distance itself.[4]

Twenty-one-year-old Jack, a recent graduate of Washington State University, loved forestry and the outdoors. The most freely outspoken of the Ford children (after the *60 Minutes* interview, he publicly admitted that he had smoked pot), he was early on quoted as saying that "I wish the whole thing with my father had never happened . . . but I'm resigned to making the best of it." Yet despite his protests, Jack was drawn to politics from the start. During the first week of the Ford Administration, Jack wrote a memo to "The President" ("Everybody else is offering advice on your staffing and future plans, so I thought I'd join the crowd") calling for "a top level post in the White House filled by a person who *happens* to be young—a position of substance with access to you." He invited George Harrison to the White House; the ex-Beatle accepted and gave Jack a button which said "OM," the Sanskrit word for wholeness. Jack went on to Utah State University, where he graduated with a major in Forestry in 1975. In 1976 he was named the director of youth marketing and special projects for Worldmark Travel Inc. Later that year, he would play an active role in his father's campaign for reelection.[5]

At age eighteen, Steve was a student at T. C. Williams High School in Alexandria. In 1976, he enrolled at California Polytechnic University as an animal science major. The one who Mrs. Ford called the "charmer" of the family—with his rugged good looks, natural charisma, and, according to his mother, his "ability to con"—would ultimately gravitate to a career in show business. However, while his father was president, a love of animals led him to complete three summers' work in Alaska on a ranch, studying grizzly bears and working on a cattle ranch and farm. Although his exploits as a cowboy made wonderful tabloid fodder, Steve did his level best to stay out of the camera's eye.[6]

With memories of Caroline Kennedy still fresh in their minds, the nation immediately embraced the First Daughter. Susan was a student at Holton Arms, a private girl's school in Bethesda, Maryland. She graduated in the summer of 1975; Holton had its senior prom at the White House, and her father spoke at her commencement exercises. Her close friend and confidant, White House photographer

David Kennerly, mentored Susan's interest in photography. In the summer of 1975, Kennerly helped her to obtain a job as a photographer on the *Capitol Journal* in Topeka. Her wit was as legendary as her mother's—of the White House, she would later describe it as "a cross between a nunnery and a penitentiary." While in the White House, she wrote a column for *Seventeen* magazine entitled "White House Diary." Her first column dealt with male chauvinism and her feelings on the press invasion of her family's privacy. She refused to give up wearing her jeans, even when her father's rather sober staffers said it made her look unladylike. In September 1975, Susan entered Mount Vernon College, a private woman's college near Washington, D.C., and the press gleefully followed her every move.[7]

On the whole, the nation liked its First Family. But virtually from the moment she set foot in the White House, it smiled along with its new first lady. Simply put, Betty Ford was fun, and she captured the public's affection in a way that no first lady, before or since, has done. She was seemingly one of them—a woman with a family much like their own, a woman who just seemed to enjoy life. Kennerly reminisced, "there are some people in this world that you like right off the bat, and Mrs. Ford is one of them. I strongly suspect that the reason is that she likes people; her affection in infectious."[8]

Anecdotes seem to serve best here. They are offered in no particular order. The first lady once stuck a lit cigarette into the hand of a statue in the Oval Office. When she crossed the International Date Line for the first time as a passenger in *Air Force One,* she gleefully wore a crown made out of tin foil and beer cans. She removed from the White House walls historic nineteenth-century wallpaper depicting battles from the American Revolution—wallpaper that had been hung in 1961 by Jacqueline Kennedy—because she found it depressing. She instructed White House chef Henry Haller on how to make the family's favorite pot roast. When he protested its parochialism—"with turnips?"—the first lady responded, "That's just the way we have it at home." One night, when Susan and two of her friends were having a sleepover in the Lincoln bedroom for the specific purpose of finding out if a ghost really inhabited the room, Mrs. Ford covered herself in a white bed sheet, glided into the room, and began reciting the Gettysburg Address, terrifying the girls. On November 17, 1975, she became the first first lady to appear on a television sitcom, when she taped an episode of the then hugely popular *Mary Tyler Moore Show*. Recorded next door to the White House at the swanky Hay-Adams Hotel (the Ford staffers did not wish to denigrate the White House by allowing in a Hollywood camera crew), Betty's few lines were the hit of the episode. And in typical Betty Ford style, she personally edited her lines until they fit her the way she wanted. (For her appearance, the first lady was paid a union scale of $172.50, which she donated to charity.) She didn't mind telling the *Washington Post* that she was an "addict" of the soap opera *The Young and the Restless*. Her chronic tardiness to meetings, banquets, and appointments irritated her husband and gave the staff fits (she would often say that "Jerry was late for our wedding and I've been making up for it ever since"), but it resounded a familiar chord with overburdened parents everywhere. She visited Studio 54, the infamous New York City nightclub that became the symbol of disco garishness. And while on a visit to Camp David, her husband was attempting to teach Liberty, the new First Dog, how to fetch. In so doing, the president leaned a bit too close to the swimming pool, and his wife pushed him in—in front of a photographer who was illustrating a book on the president.[9]

The nature of Betty Ford's personality was reflected in her parties. The other world of a first lady's existence is public entertaining, and it was a job that Mrs. Ford relished as much, if not more, than she did her public activism. All in all, she presided over some six hundred events and thirty-four state dinners—most of them in 1976 for the Bicentennial (Figure 5.1). In a distinct break from the past, each party was planned with the guest, not the hosts, in mind. Serious research was undertaken to find out the favorite entertainer of the guests and to throw the type of party that the guest would enjoy. Thus, classical pianist Van Cliburn entertained Emperor Hirohito of Japan; Singapore's Lee Kuan Yew saw the New York City Ballet; and Prime Minister and Mrs. Harold Wilson of Great Britain enjoyed opera star Beverly Sills. Also, theme dinners were established in order to highlight the tastes of the honored guest. When it was learned, for example, that President Anwar Sadat of Egypt held a fondness for the history of the American West, dinner tables were set around bronze statues by Frederic Remington. Country singer

Figure 5.1. Mrs. Ford dances with comedian Marty Allen during a White House state dinner, September 21, 1976 (courtesy of the Gerald R. Ford Library).

Johnny Cash was to entertain; however, he fell ill, and jazz singer Pearl Bailey stepped in at the last minute and delivered a bravura performance, singing one of Ford's favorite songs—"Hello Dolly"—and twirling the president around on the dance floor.[10]

Indeed, Bailey became quite special to the first lady. The two women met for the first time on Betty's fifty-seventh birthday (April 8, 1975) at the Kennedy Center. The two of them hit it off immediately, breaking into song backstage. At a subsequent dinner, she joined Bailey onstage to sing the Michigan fight song. The jazz singer became particular friends with the First Family. At one party, she danced a spirited Charleston with the president; she publicly referred to the first lady as "my sister, Betty Ford." In 1975, Ford appointed Bailey as a special ambassador to the United Nations; she would serve in that capacity during the rest of the Ford Administration, as well as that of Ronald Reagan and George H. W. Bush.[11]

Maria Downs, Mrs. Ford's third social secretary, remembered that when she was hired in the fall 1975, Betty had been doing the job herself for a number of months, and "I had the feeling that [she] was enjoying this." In an unpublished memoir, Downs labeled social life in the Ford White House as "relaxed but correct." The emphasis, however, was decidedly on the relaxed. The Fords broke away from the regal nature of the White House dinner that had dominated the Nixon scene. (Mrs. Ford's mentor, Martha Graham, would chirp about those days: "That was a dreary time. A vicious time. I couldn't come here then.") Betty Ford had been a partier in her youth in New York City, and she had enjoyed a fast-paced social life in Grand Rapids. She and her husband still enjoyed a good bash. She thought of the White House she inherited and concluded, "This home has been a grave. I want it to sing."[12]

Sing it did. Formal functions at the Ford White House became rollicking celebrations, with a decided emphasis on dancing and having a good time. Unpredictability became the watchword when going to the White House during the Ford years. Violinist Ernest Fodor performed; so did country crooner Tennessee Ernie Ford. At one party, guests were stunned to see Supreme Court Justice William O. Douglas, who, as minority leader, Ford had tried to impeach. At another, Katherine Graham, the scion of the *Washington Post* and the scourge of the Nixon White House, made her first appearance at a state dinner in almost a decade (she quipped, "It's marvelous—all the underground is here"). And they danced the night away, with the president and first lady often outlasting the honored guests at the party. At one affair, when Mrs. Ford could not get her husband to leave the party even at the advanced hour of 1:15 AM, she groused to a reporter, "He's very irresponsible." There were also changes of a more significant nature. Ford himself expressed a desire to have more young people at White House dinners, a wish that instantly became social policy. The Fords also changed the policy of having unmarried, divorced, or widowed persons attend White House dinners alone; now they could bring an escort. The first lady was also not above using her parties for politicking. Most famously, she returned to the use of round tables at White House dinners because more women could be seated at them than at a traditional dais.[13]

But the Fords' new style of entertaining was not without its critics. When Ford entertained the Shah of Iran in May 1975, for example, the entertainment drew some flak in the press. Actress Ann-Margret ended her Las Vegas revue in a scanty red, white, and blue costume and was hoisted up in it by dancers until she touched an

East Room chandelier. The press had a field day; the mildest criticism called the actress's show inappropriate. The first lady, however, had a ready explanation for the choice: "We picked her because the Shah of Iran likes pretty women. And so does my husband." And when the White House included the popular singing duo The Captain and Tennille to perform for Queen Elizabeth II and Prince Philip of Great Britain, the performers were criticized for performing a so-called provocative song: "Muskrat Love" (indeed, the duo had not been the first choice of the White House; when headliner Bob Hope was unable to deliver Bing Crosby as his costar, he asked the musicians to fill in). The most notable criticism, however, came when the Emperor and Empress of Japan were welcomed to the White House for the first time since World War II. Voices from all over the political spectrum decried the invitation, noting that Japan's complicity for World War II could not be danced away during a party. Yet such criticism was short-lived. To the vast majority of Americans, the Fords of Grand Rapids were the perfect hosts.[14]

Like many of the things that happened during the Ford Administration, their biggest party was also an inherited one. Most of the planning for the nation's two hundredth birthday party had been undertaken during the Nixon Administration, but this did not stop the Fords from basking in reflected glory. Gerald Ford felt that the Bicentennial was one of the most important moments of his presidency. Certainly it offered a unique political opportunity—the Fourth of July celebrations were made to order for showing the president as leader of the free world, and only days before the Republican nominating convention. Tall ships sailed in New York Harbor, the Liberty Bell rang for the first time in decades, and Ford appeared in patriotic scenes that would have made Frank Capra tear up. He and his wife also showed themselves perfectly able to dance with royalty. The visit of Queen Elizabeth and Prince Philip during the Bicentennial Week was one of the most lavish affairs of the 1970s—despite the sacrilegious playing of "Muskrat Love."

For her part, aside from serving as hostess at the several state dinners, the first lady was confined to a very limited role during the Bicentennial celebration. She served on no committee that dealt specifically with the celebration, and she made few public appearances without her husband that were Bicentennial related. Perhaps this was because the West Wing feared that her often-polarizing presence would draw attention away from ceremonies that could easily be spun as evidence that the nation's wounds had been bound; perhaps it was because they did not wish to risk an incident so close to the nominating convention. Her most notable solo appearance was in June 1976, when she joined Nancy Kissinger and Joan Kennedy in Plymouth, Massachusetts, to open a Bicentennial exhibition about Revolutionary-era women called Remember the Ladies. The exhibit included pictures of the leading women of the period, including Abigail Adams and Martha Washington. Mrs. Ford, however, expressed regret when she learned that the famous Molly Pitcher had never really existed, because "I received the Molly Pitcher Award once."[15]

Gerald Ford noted in his inaugural address the nation "had not chosen me by secret ballot." From virtually the moment he took office, however, he was planning to change that. On August 21, 1974, Ford authorized his press secretary, Jerald terHorst, to tell reporters that he would "probably" run in 1976. But as he remembered in his memoirs, "the decision wasn't final then—I still had Betty to convince." Ford maintains that he "fully intended to honor" the pledge he made to his wife in 1973—to get out of politics and retire in 1977— "but Betty released me from it." Neither Ford wrote about any such discussion. Mrs. Ford did tell an interviewer in late 1974 that if her husband wanted to run, "then I would accept it. He knows best about these things." After her cancer surgery, she faced questions about whether or not her health would cause the president to drop out of the race; each time, she made it clear that she supported him, going so far as to quip in August 1975 that he would not be running "unless I wanted him to." But one cannot help but believe that the decision was made from the start, and without much input from his wife. Sheila Weidenfeld remembered the first lady's reaction to her husband's formal announcement of his candidacy: "Oh God, what *else* is new?"[16]

On November 20, 1975, to the surprise of virtually no one, Ronald Reagan announced that he would challenge the president for the Republican nomination. Initially, the Ford campaign did not take the Reagan challenge seriously enough. Ford's team utilized a "Rose

Garden strategy," wherein the candidate would stay in Washington and be president while surrogates went on the road in his name. Within the framework of this strategy, in spite of their long-held concerns over her unpredictability, Ford's staff was forced to concede the first lady's popularity. Howard "Bo" Calloway, then the chairman of the President Ford Committee, wrote Weidenfeld in September 1975 that he had been on the road for two weeks, and had, to no one's surprise, fielded many questions about the *60 Minutes* interview. But when he asked fellow Republicans if Betty Ford was available, would they want her to visit their district, "I'm happy to report that in every case, the answer was an enthusiastic 'yes.'" The research of Robert Teeter and Stuart Spencer told the campaign what the polls had already shown—that "large majorities approve of Mrs. Ford's performance as First Lady and see her in a positive light."[17]

Thus, Betty Ford became the Ford campaign's chief surrogate in the primary season; she described herself to a reporter as a "cheerful volunteer worker." However, this type of volunteerism necessitated her muting her passion for topics that did not play well before the New Right. In New Hampshire, she downplayed her work on the ERA as well as her victory over cancer, and concentrated instead on making vague statements in favor of her husband. At almost every stop, there were protesters opposing her stand on ERA and her stand on abortion (both Reagans were equally public supporters of the prolife stand). But even in conservative New Hampshire, the supporters always outnumbered the protesters. It was, after all, a state which, despite the rabid opposition of the *Manchester Union-Leader*, had not only ratified the ERA, but had only recently passed a similar state measure. Thus, the ground was fertile for a visit from the first lady. At a stop in Durham, 3,500 University of New Hampshire students seemed to politely tolerate the president, but when Mrs. Ford was introduced, she was given a thunderous standing ovation. One of the hottest items in the campaign were the buttons that read "Betty's Husband for President." In the ultimate homage to her popularity, *Washington Post* political cartoonist Herblock sketched a befuddled New Hampshire voter, scratching his head, asking "could I write in a first name—like Betty?" Quite aside from her popularity, her presence in the campaign changed the rules of engagement for all political spouses; as a result of Betty's candor, they were all being asked tougher, more policy-laden questions—a fact that many of them bemoaned quite frequently.[18]

And yet the New Hampshire campaign saw a serious, and potentially damaging, public schism between the president and the first lady. The abortion issue had first appeared as a problem for the White House with the nomination for vice president of Nelson Rockefeller, who supported liberal abortion laws while he was governor of New York and vetoed legislation designed to overturn those laws. Then in May 1975, *Newsday* reported that the Defense Department had been authorizing abortions—nearly 5,400 in 1974—for women in military services and the wives and daughters of servicemen. This policy was based on a 1972 Executive Order signed by Nixon, which permitted abortions in cases where physical or mental health was threatened. The American Civil Liberties Union was concerned that the order conflicted with the 1973 decision of the Supreme Court in *Roe v. Wade.* Others were concerned that *any* form of sanctioned abortion might violate the laws of the country where the serviceman might be stationed. However, some quick staff work found that Nixon had, in fact, issued a statement rather than an order, thus allowing the Pentagon to reverse the policy without involving Ford. For his part, Ford tried to straddle the issue by saying that he was against abortion as a moral issue, but wanted to leave the matter strictly up to the states.[19]

The issue simmered on the political back burner until the Reagan challenge rekindled it; it was made to order for the New Right. In 1976, Illinois Congressman Henry Hyde mounted the first serious legislative attack against *Roe v. Wade.* His proposed legislation would deny the use of Medicaid funds for abortions, even when the mother's life was in danger. Such legislation would effectively deny to a poor woman a right guaranteed her under *Roe* that might be exercised by a woman who could afford such services. Ford vetoed the measure. However, it was passed over his veto in 1976.

The abortion issue was complicated by Betty's clear prochoice stand. Although both Fords were in agreement that the Hyde Amendment should be defeated, they clearly disagreed on the issue of abortion. Mrs. Ford's prochoice belief was clear, and had been stated many times to the press, even as recently as January 1976, when she told *Time* magazine, "I feel it is the right of a human being to make her own decisions." Ford had dodged the issue of abortion throughout his presidency. But now, with his wife's forthright statement to the press in an election year, he was forced to clarify his own position. On January 16, he announced that he favored an amendment that would let each state decide for itself on the issue, and that both Fords supported the right to obtain an abortion in limited situations such as rape or illness, but not on demand.[20]

Thus, Betty Ford's disagreement with her husband became campaign fodder. When asked about his wife's views by an audience member later that month in New Hampshire, Ford quipped that, "as you know, my dear wife took another position on that." Many complained that once again, the first lady had inserted her opinions into the political arena where they did not belong. Yet there were others, like columnist Nicholas von Hoffman, who concluded that the "disagreement" was a set-up, allowing the Fords to have it both ways and to court both the prochoice and the prolife vote. Hoffman concluded that "it must be assumed that she is, knowingly or unknowingly, being used by her husband's political managers to allow him to work both sides of the street."[21]

Ford's victory in New Hampshire was narrow, and Reagan was far from defeated. Indeed, the governor defiantly told aides, who pled with him to withdraw from the race, that he would stay in the race until the convention. This turned out to be a wise move. Reagan won the North Carolina primary on the strength of his criticism of Ford's foreign policy. He went on to win primaries throughout the South and Midwest, turning the last weeks of the primary campaign into the closest contest in decades.[22]

The Ford campaign was now taking Reagan very seriously indeed. Nevertheless, it continued to resist the temptation to put their candidate on the road. Thus, surrogates were even more needed. Mike and Gayle Ford did not campaign, Steven did so only on the rarest of occasions, and the teenaged Susan was constrained from traveling except at the side of one of her parents. Jack, however, threw himself into the fray with vigor. Doing a complete reversal on his earlier disdain for his lot, Jack found that he actually enjoyed active campaigning. A born politician and a good speaker who had worked in the 1972 Nixon campaign, Jack was a natural on the "rubber chicken circuit" (one of his favorite after-dinner lines: "I went through the 200 nights a year that Dad was traveling for the Republican party, and I'd hate to see it go down the drain"). He longed to offer policy ideas, but those ideas were spurned by the campaign's inner circle. Frustrated when his ideas were not taken seriously by the campaign, Jack nevertheless stayed with the campaign until the bitter end.[23]

Yet throughout the later primaries, it was Betty Ford who continued to bear the lion's share of the campaigning for her husband. Her popularity was such that the crowds she drew often were larger than those drawn by her husband. Indeed, the West Wing was so enamored of her contribution that she received something that no other first lady had received: her own speechwriter. In February 1976, Mary Frances Pullen was detailed to the East Wing staff. A native of Tennessee, Pullen had been a television reporter and an editorial writer for the *Commercial Appeal,* and she had worked as a film producer for an advertising agency. Since April 1974, she had been serving as a speechwriter for the Republican National Committee in Washington. Before she was done, Mrs. Ford's twenty-eight-person staff—nine of whom worked full-time just to answer the first lady's mail—was the largest staff in the history of first ladies.[24]

Mrs. Ford effectively canceled the White House social schedule, and from March to August, she took to the road. She continued to avoid the controversial issues that had become her hallmark, causing Weidenfeld to privately complain in mid-March that "Mrs. Ford hasn't done anything that means anything in so long," and that the campaign had caused "a throwback . . . to [Betty's] old life, the political wife syndrome that drove her to a psychiatrist in the first place." She was, however, a "gamer." On April 3, she appeared at the annual press dinner at the Gridiron Club. After newsmen had serenaded her with "Once in Love with Betty," she came onstage in a full-length ball gown and did an impromptu soft-shoe that brought down the house.[25]

A classic bit of campaign shtick introduced Betty Ford as trucker. The early 1970s saw the height of America's love affair with citizen's band (CB) radios. A technology lifted from the trucking industry, which used the low-wattage radios to communicate with each other while on the road, truckers talked through a thinly veiled incognito, called "handles"—each trucker had one and used it to tell his "good buddies" on the road where the state troopers ("County Mounties") were lying in wait with their radar guns. As more and more passenger vehicles began to carry CB radios, they became a cultural phenomenon. In 1976, Susan got her mother one of her own. There was a small hue and cry when it was learned that the first lady was issued her temporary license with remarkable speed (to solve the minicrisis, the Federal Communication Commission immediately decided that temporary licenses would now instantly be issued to all applicants). There was also a protest when it was learned that she used the radio to contact truckers and cajole them to vote for her husband (when she went on the road to campaign, the Secret Service rigged her radio so she could operate it out of a suitcase). Nevertheless, the first lady, who now sported the handle "First Mama," immensely enjoyed herself on her CB, radioing truckers on Interstate 95 as they raced within miles of the White House.[26]

Despite such moments, the campaign took an obvious physical toll on the first lady. Early on, a reporter observed that she "seemed very low-key and tired, which immediately led to speculation that her cancer had reoccurred and rekindled talk of Ford's quitting." Such speculation was groundless, but Mrs. Ford was clearly being brutalized by the campaign trail. The hotly contested Florida campaign, coming on the heels of the North Carolina defeat, was particularly grueling. At its end (a primary that Ford won), she was physically exhausted, a fact that did not go unmentioned by the press. An official White House statement simply said that she was tired from the previous week's campaigning in Florida and suffering from "a little stiffness in her neck."[27] But a description of her by a reporter who saw her campaign in Florida bears quoting at length:

> As one sees the wretched Mrs. Ford lurch almost drunkenly from appointment to dreary appointment, her teeth gritted in a bone-crashing contortion that is said to be a smile, her voice lisping with the sound of ill-fitting dentures, her hair piled untidily on her head, like a Grand Housewife suddenly called upon to entertain the factory boss, one begins to feel that she is being used, exploited, and driven for the unashamed purpose of President Ford's campaign.[28]

On occasion, Mrs. Ford also let fatigue allow her candor to get the better of her. In June, Congressman Wayne Hays of Ohio admitted to having an affair with a paid member of his staff who had done virtually no work. When asked to comment on the story, she referred to Hays as a "very fine gentleman, and he wasn't married when it happened." The Ford campaign put out an immediate release, saying that the first lady had been misquoted, but she refused to back down. She told the press that White House press secretary Ron Nessen, who issued the clarification, was mistaken: "He is a very fine gentleman . . . and I probably did call him a fine gentleman." As the campaign ground on, she also looked for a scapegoat for her husband's defeats. In June, she blamed Bo Callaway for the surprising number of primary losses, calling him "complacent."[29]

Of the many draining moments in the campaign, one stands out, not only for the toll it must have taken on Mrs. Ford, but as a further example of her courage. On June 22, the first lady was at the New York Hilton Hotel, attending the Jewish National Fund Dinner. She was there as a favor to Milton Hoffman, who had donated a room to one of her favorite causes, Washington's Hospital for Sick Children. The purpose of the dinner was to raise funds for an American Bicentennial Park to be built in Jerusalem. Presiding over the event was the Fund's president, Dr. Maurice Sage. Sage was to give the first lady an ornate Bible from Jerusalem, but immediately before the presentation, he began to stumble. He collapsed on the stage while reaching into his pocket. Sage was having a heart attack, and as he fell, he was trying to reach his nitroglycerin tablets. Mrs. Ford moved from the podium and back to her seat as doctors who had been in the audience attended to Sage. She reached out to comfort Martin Hoffman, son of her friend Milton, by patting him on the back. Then, as efforts were made behind her to resuscitate the rabbi, the crowd edged toward panic. She moved back to the podium. Her voice noticeably trembling, she asked the spectators to "Bow our heads for a moment for Dr. Sage . . . he is going to the hospital and needs our prayers. Would you rise and bow your heads?" Mrs. Ford led the now-stunned audience in prayer: "I'll have to say it in my own words. Dear Father in heaven, we ask thy blessing on this magnificent man, Dr. Sage. We know you can take care of him, we know You can bring him back to us, we know You are our leader and our strength." The first lady was then escorted out of the hotel; Sage died an hour later at the hospital.[30]

Up to the convening of the Republican convention, the issue of who would win the primary was still in doubt, because Reagan won many of the later primaries. In the final weeks, the Ford campaign narrowed the gap by a shrewd use of the incumbency, as the president personally telephoned hundreds of delegates, invited them to the White House, and made astute use of political promises. The first lady joined in, heavily working the phones herself, as she called selected delegates to cement their vote—this time not lobbying for a cause, but for her husband. At the site of the convention, Kansas City's Kemper Arena, she was once more called upon to show the flag. In what was billed as a "Battle of the Spouses," Nancy Reagan first appeared to the applause of the crowd. Then Mrs. Ford appeared, and the applause that met her appearance was thunderous. She even danced for the crowd, doing a turn with entertainer Tony Orlando to the strains of his hit song, "Tie a Yellow Ribbon 'Round the Old Oak Tree." The following night, she was introduced to the convention by actor Cary Grant, who quipped that it would be good for women if there were a "further four years" of "pillow talk" in the White House.[31]

After finally winning the nomination, Ford once again found himself the underdog. This time, he trailed former Georgia Governor Jimmy Carter by twenty points. As a result, there was a shift in strategy within the Ford campaign. Still using the Rose Garden strategy (what one participant now called the "No-Campaign Campaign"), the Ford campaign continued to keep the president in Washington as much as possible. However, the focus of their advertising would now be shifted to show him not as "presidential," but as a family man (one ad: "sometimes a man's family can say a lot about the man").[32]

In what was perhaps the biggest mistake of the fall campaign, the "No-Campaign" strategy grounded the first lady. In a complete reversal from the successful primary strategy, Mrs. Ford was hardly used in the fall campaign and she disappeared from serious news coverage, a vantage point she had occupied throughout the primaries. The Ford Campaign's *Fact Book,* a collection of information

Figure 5.2. Mrs. Ford reads President Ford's concession speech, White House
Press Briefing Room, November 3, 1976. Behind Mrs. Ford, left to right:
Steven Ford, President Ford, Mike Ford, Gayle Ford
(courtesy of the Gerald R. Ford Library).

compiled in September 1976 and given to campaign surrogates, includes only a perfunctory fourteen-sentence biography of the first
lady that does not mention her cancer operation, her support for
the ERA, or the *60 Minutes* interview. Instead, it notes that in the
1950s and 1960s, she "concentrated on her husband and family." Of
her almost two years as first lady, it said only that she had "new responsibilities." She would campaign only sporadically until the
middle of October—an ill-advised decision that kept one of the
Ford campaign's best campaigners out of commission until it was
too late.[33]

On November 3, 1976, Gerald Ford lost his bid to be elected to
his own term as president. During the last hectic days of campaigning, he completely lost his voice. As a result, it was Betty
Ford, standing next to her husband and surrounded by her children, who was called upon to read the traditional telegram of concession and congratulations to the new president-elect. She was
stoic, speaking slowly, never wavering from the script of the telegram, and only occasionally looking up at the camera (Figure 5.2).

Ron Nessen observed that Ford had "a terrible look of hurt and bewilderment in his eyes. He didn't understand why he'd been turned out of office. Those who saw the look on his face that day will never forget it."[34]

After the telegram was read, the First Family took no questions. They simply turned and left.[35]

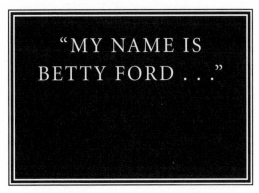

CHAPTER 6

"MY NAME IS BETTY FORD ..."

Betty Ford was happy to be rid of Washington. In an interview with Barbara Walters broadcast on January 2, 1977, she mused that although she would have been "perfectly willing to serve the country for four more years," she was "happy because I was getting my husband back." On inauguration day, 1977, the former first lady joked with reporters that "I can hardly wait to go to that nice warm weather." Immediately after the election, the Fords had decided not to return to Virginia. Instead, they sold their Alexandria home and purchased one on the Thunderbird Golf Club in Rancho Mirage, California, just outside of Palm Springs. During the interview with Walters, the Fords kidded about the move—the president saying it was because it was "good for Betty's health," and his wife playfully reminding her husband that "it also has twenty-four golf courses." It was a neighborhood for the rich and famous—their neighbors included the Frank Sinatras, the Bob Hopes, the Walter Annenbergs, and even the Spiro Agnews. Mrs. Ford was wistful: "This must have been what the Garden of Eden looked like."[1]

Although she maintained that she expected to keep busy with volunteer work, and fund-raising drives for cancer research and the performing arts, Mrs. Ford expected to settle with her husband into retirement from politics. Indeed, she had been promised that would be the case. Yet although Ford did not immediately reenter the political arena, he did hit the fund-raising, lecture, and golf tournament circuits. One estimate would have the former president earning a half million dollars per year for his labors. Soon he was gone from home as often as when he had been a congressman.[2]

While in the White House, Betty Ford had become accustomed to at least having her husband home at night. Now, she was once again a political widow. And she did not have her family around her, as she had during the congressional and vice presidential years. All had grown into lives of their own. Even Susan was no longer at home, having withdrawn from Mount Vernon College and transferred to the University of Kansas in January 1977. To be sure, Betty had tasks. She had been contracted to write her memoirs, as well as to make a few media appearances. And there were substantive appearances that continued Mrs. Ford's support for the cause of equal rights for women. In November 1977, Mrs. Ford, Lady Bird Johnson, and first lady Rosalynn Carter shared a Houston stage together at the opening ceremony of the National Women's Conference to celebrate the International Women's Year that Mrs. Ford's husband had declared from the White House only two years before. (Each woman accepted a torch that had been run to Houston from Seneca Falls.) This seminal event would become a key target of Phyllis Schlafly's ire as the fight over the Equal Rights Amendment steamed into its final legislative stages. But for all intents and purposes, Betty Ford was once again home alone. Thus, as she remembered, "I had to adjust to a completely different lifestyle. I found that more stressful than the pressures I had to deal with in the White House." She dropped weight at an alarming rate. She would regularly keep her nightgown on until the very late morning hours. She was forgetting things. She would fall asleep in the middle of conversations. No doubt with a sigh, Susan remembered, "She had no friends. You couldn't trust her. . . . I feared she would fall and crack her head open. She was walking into a dead-end street." As Mrs. Ford remembered it, she was a "nice dopey pill-pusher, sitting around nodding."[3]

In a later article, Betty Ford claimed, "my problems developed after January 20, 1977." This is simply not true. As we have seen, the genesis of her "problems" lay with the alcoholism of her father, and may well have been made worse by the alcoholism of her first husband. Since she was already at risk, the Washington social scene during her husband's tenure in Congress, as well as to the prescription of painkillers for a pinched nerve, joined with her feelings of loneliness and abandonment to make her addiction more acute. This led to a nervous breakdown and psychiatric treatment—all before her husband was nominated for the vice presidency. There is evidence to suggest that after being thrust onto the national stage, her "problem" was less visible, but as much evidence—slurring of speech, regular cocktail party attendance, missing of appointments—suggests, it was by no means in remission. Despite her attempt to pitch it otherwise, throughout the White House years, Betty Ford had a problem. However, once she and her husband arrived at their new home in Rancho Mirage in 1977, Mrs. Ford was back in the same position she had been in in the 1960s—alone, and with feelings of abandonment. She drank more and took more pills than she had probably done while in the White House and under the ever-watchful camera's eye. She later remembered that she was now popping all sorts of "gourmet medications. . . . I had pills to go to sleep, pills for pain, pills to counteract the reactions of all the other pills. And each of these, please note, was from a doctor's prescription." She also remembered that she saw her physician weekly because of her arthritis, but that "he was unaware or didn't want to recognize my dependency on the drugs. I don't think he knew anything about my use of alcohol."[4]

Much of the nation saw evidence of her illness for the first time in 1977. Mrs. Ford had contracted with NBC-TV to go to the Soviet Union and narrate a performance of *The Nutcracker Suite* by the Bolshoi Ballet. She did so, but what the public saw was a narrator who slurred her words and looked as if she were half asleep. She later addressed the press criticism of her performance: "They were right. I was so overmedicated." By April 1978, she felt that "I was dying, and everyone knew it but me." Yet unlike 1965, when she spiraled into a breakdown, this time her family stepped in.[5]

In 1993, Betty Ford wryly noted that "when a family is living with alcoholism, it's like having an elephant in the living room: everybody walks around the beast, but nobody does anything." This had absolutely been the case for the Ford family. It took almost two decades of addiction, and almost two years of life outside of politics, for the

Ford family to admit to themselves that she needed help (Figure 6.1). Ultimately, it was Susan, not her father, who planned and initiated the two interventions in the spring of 1978 that saved her mother's life. Dr. Joseph Cruise, Mrs. Ford and Susan's gynecologist and himself a recovering alcoholic, had obtained Susan's services to take pictures of a rehabilitation center, so as to help raise money for it. On the way to the photo shoot, Susan told Cruise about her mother's behavior, and Cruise recommended an intervention. The idea was pitched to Ford, but he was not immediately in favor of it (as biographer James Cannon noted, "he never was one as a congressman to initiate things"). But before he could make up his mind, Cruise and Susan staged their own intervention, with the help of the Ford family housekeeper and Mrs. Ford's secretary. The result, as Susan remembered it, was that her mother "called me a monster and kicked me out of the house." For Ford, having his daughter treated in such a way was the turning point in his view of his wife's addiction; he would remember that he now felt that "the risk was worth taking."[6]

On April 1, having been hastily crash-trained by Cruise in intervention therapy, Betty Ford's entire family faced her. Her husband, who had prevailed upon Henry Kissinger to pinch-hit for him at several speaking engagements, ran the intervention, a decision that surprised all present. Sitting in a semicircle in front of her, each in turn told her that they believed her to be an addict, and what her addictions had personally done to them. Steve told her of a recent incident where he came home with a date, and his mother would not come to dinner; rather, "she sat in front of the television, and kept on drinking." Gayle Ford admitted that while she hoped for children of her own, she believed that her mother-in-law would not be a fit grandmother.[7]

Mrs. Ford remembered: "I listened, but I didn't hear that they loved me. I heard that I had failed." As soon as the intervention was over, she got dressed, and then immediately swallowed several pills ("I'd show them. They were going to confiscate my supply?"). After that last act of defiance, she stayed at home for one week, under a doctor's care, to detoxify. On April 8—her sixtieth birthday—she had dinner at the home of former Ambassador Leonard Firestone, a close family friend. Two days later, she checked into Long Beach Naval Hospital's Alcohol and Drug Rehabilitation Service. Susan

Figure 6.1. The Ford family. First row, left to right: First Lady Betty Ford,
President Gerald R. Ford. Second row, left to right: Steve Ford, Susan Ford, Jack
Ford, Gayle Ford, and Mike Ford (courtesy of the Gerald R. Ford Library).

would later claim that if her mother had not gone into treatment,
the family had a backup plan: "We would have told her, Mother, you
won't see us again."[8]

Betty Ford's adjustment to life at Long Beach was traumatic. In
her own words, she "considered herself a very special person who
had been married to a President of the United States, and I didn't
think I should have to discuss my personal problems with just any-
body." She remembered being led into a room with four beds, and
with other women's clothes on the beds. "I balked," she remembered. "I wasn't going to sign in. The doctor said, 'Well, Mrs. Ford, if
you insist on a private room, I'll have these other ladies moved out.'
He had me pegged beautifully." Mrs. Ford stayed put, but her demands for divalike treatment (Cruise remembered that she was "a
little cocksure") were less important than the fact that she had yet to
admit that she was an alcoholic. When the former first lady was admitted to Long Beach, it was reported that she was only battling an
addiction to painkillers. The reasons for this were, in her mind, simple. She later remembered that she told her doctors that it would
embarrass her husband if it were admitted that she was an alcoholic,

and also she believed that her addiction to alcohol "wasn't dramatic." However, on April 15, Steve Ford told a reporter that his mother was seeking treatment for both drug and alcohol abuse. As Mrs. Ford remembered it, she "wasn't prepared to sign off on that." This forced the issue, and precipitated a second intervention, ten days into her treatment. Ford participated again in the intervention and heard his wife proclaim, "If you're going to call me an alcoholic, I won't stand for it." Yet faced with the reality of the situation, she began to worry that when news of her alcoholism was publicly confirmed, it would embarrass her husband—a fear that he immediately laid to rest by informing her that it did not embarrass him in the least, and by penning a statement that said she was at Long Beach for drugs and alcohol. Two weeks after her admission to Long Beach, Betty Ford admitted she was an alcoholic; she was released after twenty-eight days.[9]

In July 1979, in a show of support for his wife, Gerald Ford stopped drinking.[10]

Only a fraction of Betty Ford's famous recovery from her substance addictions was physical in nature. Tina Mion, an Arizona artist, has painted fifty-three striking portraits of each of the first ladies. Her 1999 study of Betty Ford, entitled "The Other Side of Betty Ford: Six of Diamonds," is taken liberally from photos that depict the first lady dancing at the May 7th College of Art in Peking while visiting China with her husband in December 1975 (Figure 6.2). What sets this portrait apart is the figure of Gerald Ford in the background. He is watching his wife dance; she is contentedly unaware of his presence.[11]

After her stay at Long Beach, Betty Ford inched closer to reclaiming complete control of her life. For her family, this led to some unexpected complications. Betty remembered that when she was what she described as a "practicing alcoholic," the family could easily manipulate her—"I'd say yes to practically anything." But after her treatment, "I took control of my life. At first there was a lot of resentment that I suddenly wanted to be in charge again. They had to realize this was a healthy person and this was what recovery was all about."[12]

For many Americans, the most outward sign of this new independence came within months of her release. In September 1978, she announced that she had had a face-lift (an event that is barely discussed

Figure 6.2. "The Other Side of Betty Ford: Six of Diamonds"
(Tina Mion, artist; photograph of painting by Paul Ruchea).

in her memoirs). Indeed, she announced it before she went in for the procedure, convinced that if she didn't, the public would think she was getting further cancer surgery or substance abuse therapy. She tried to downplay her decision to reporter Helen Thomas: "Isn't it wonderful? I'm sixty years old and I need a new face?" But the amount of mail that she received from a public believing that she should grow older without altering her body was surprising. However, the former first lady was sanguine about the reaction: "Now are we going to go through all the hair transplants and name some of the politicians who had cosmetic work done? I think it's just jealousy. I prefer to grow old looking as well as I possibly can." Comedian Bob Hope quipped, "the only new face in the Republican Party."[13]

Also in 1978, what would become the first volume of Mrs. Ford's memoirs was published. *The Times of My Life* was in galleys before she entered treatment. One of the first things she did upon her release (although it took some coaxing) was to add a final chapter entitled "Long Beach." The following year, Mrs. Ford also publicly responded to the publication of a memoir written by a member of her staff. Sheila Weidenfeld's *First Lady's Lady: With the Fords at the White House* has the distinction of being one of the first of what would be a long line of kiss-and-tell books written by White House employees. Much of Weidenfeld's substantial evidence of the second-class treatment that the first lady's press operation received from the West Wing is lost in a barrage of insider anecdotes about the people in the Ford White House. Few of them are flattering portraits, but the stories about the Ford children—that Susan had dated a married man and that her mother knew about it; that Jack had used marijuana; and that Steve had brought a date home to the White House and slept with her in the Queen's Bedroom—particularly angered Mrs. Ford. Without challenging the truthfulness of Weidenfeld's claims, she told reporter Myra MacPherson that "to write about children who have lived or are living in the White House is a very unfair sort of thing, particularly when it is critical. To take things that have been confided, really, and put them in print, I think, is very bad." She also took umbrage at claims in the book that Weidenfeld had somehow molded Mrs. Ford as first lady: "Actually, I didn't see much of Sheila. That she produced me is far from the truth. Sheila *wanted* to, but she was not allowed to."[14]

But more important than any of this was the fact that Mrs. Ford had found a project for herself—one that would be hers, not her husband's. She hinted at this venture at the end of *Times of My Life,* when she wrote, almost casually: "Eisenhower Hospital in Palm Springs is planning an active program for chemically addicted patients . . . I'll be able to participate, to help others."[15]

Soon after her release from Long Beach, Mrs. Ford had lunch with Leonard Firestone, a close friend and a recovering alcoholic himself. About a year earlier, Firestone's wife, along with Gerald and Betty Ford, had organized an intervention (Firestone remembered that Mrs. Ford had told him, "one alcoholic can't fool another alcoholic") that sent Firestone back into rehab for the second time, where he successfully completed the program. Now, like the former first lady, he wanted to give something back. Firestone wanted to create a program at the Eisenhower Hospital; Mrs. Ford, who bemoaned the fact that when she started her treatment at Long Beach, "most of us women had to participate in male-oriented programs," wanted to address the gender inequity inherent in the treatment programs of the day. Thus were the wheels put into motion for what would become a singular medical facility—one that the two friends were ready to build.[16]

For some time, Joe Cruise had been lobbying the Eisenhower Medical Center in Palm Springs to add a substance abuse rehabilitation facility. Walter Annenberg, then a member of the Eisenhower

Center's board of trustees, suggested to both Mrs. Ford and to Firestone that the two of them begin a fund-raising project that would bring the type of facility that they envisioned to the Eisenhower Center. For Mrs. Ford, one of the keys was that the new center would not discriminate—either overtly in the number of beds provided, or covertly in the type of treatment offered—against women. This was an important issue because in 1989, only a third of those in America who sought help for alcoholism were women. Indeed, this would remain a hobbyhorse for the former first lady for years to come. She continued to argue, as she did on ABC's *Good Morning America* in January 2002: "Women have always been discriminated against in many fields, but particularly in the addiction field. In the very beginning, it was like only men had this problem. And women were pretty much hidden by their families."[17]

The fund-raising for the rehab center began in earnest in 1978, when Mrs. Ford was amending the first volume of her memoirs. It was to be a difficult undertaking; even though she was no longer taking tranquilizers, she still suffered from her pinched nerve, and the pain could be excruciating. Nevertheless, Cruise's project was literally just what the doctor ordered. Now, for the first time in her life, Betty Ford had a project—a goal—that was completely independent of her husband. Particularly with the help of her friend Dolores Hope, Mrs. Ford became a fund-raiser extraordinaire. By 1981, they had already raised $3 million.[18]

However, the fund-raising almost came to an abrupt end in the summer of 1980. Since 1979, Ford had been putting out feelers to the Republican Party, testing the waters for a possible presidential candidacy for himself the following year, thus setting up a rematch between himself and Jimmy Carter. For her part, the former first lady remained aloof, telling a reporter that if "circumstances" led her husband to run, she would support him with "all love and conviction." However, "I would hate for Jerry to run and have him defeated." Ford eventually took himself out of the presidential race. But in one of the most bizarre courtships in modern American politics, Ronald Reagan—then guaranteed the Republican nomination for the presidency, sent out feelers to Ford, asking him if he would be interested in running with Reagan as his vice presidential candidate. The negotiations, spearheaded by Henry Kissinger, centered on a vague construction of a "copresidency," in which Ford would play an infinitely more significant role than had been played in past vice presidencies. The end came during an interview with Walter Cronkite, where Ford let the cat out of the bag too early and denied Reagan his surprise announcement. An angry Reagan withdrew the offer. Mrs. Ford breathed a sigh of relief: "I was more than grateful for the way it played out. My new life in recovery was precious to me and I was glad to be done with politics."[19]

On October 3, 1982, the Betty Ford Center at the Eisenhower Medical Center was dedicated. Vice President George Bush, Leonard Firestone, Joe Cruise, Bob and Dolores Hope, and Gerald Ford all spoke. During his speech, Ford broke down and cried. Beginning its life as a corporate part of the Eisenhower Center, less than a year later, it became an independent subsidiary of the Eisenhower Medical Center. It had its own hospital license, board, and budget. Founded as a 102-bed recovery center, the Betty Ford Center saved—then and now—50 percent of its space for women and 50 percent for men. Depending on the patient, the program lasts between four and twelve weeks, and costs $16,500 for an average stay of twenty-eight days.[20]

Betty Ford had not wanted the Center named after herself. (She would later recall her hesitation: "Of course I didn't want my name on it. Why would I? What if I couldn't stay sober? It would be a big embarrassment.") She changed her mind however, because "as my name was on there, it was a safe place for women to come and be treated." The day after the dedication, the Betty Ford Center admitted their first patients—two men, and two women. That same day, they opened their Intensive Family Treatment Program—a requirement, novel for the time, where the families of the patients attend a series of lectures and therapy on their own for a week.[21]

With the founding of the center that bore her name, Betty Ford had finally broken free of her husband's ambitions. They were as intimately close as ever, and they seemed to have no qualms with public displays of affection. Yet that had always been the case, and Mrs. Ford had chosen to give herself wholly to her husband's career, with tragic results for herself. Now, while Ford traveled, spoke, and advised, she carved out her own path. She was completely independent, by choice, of her husband's career for the first time in her life.

The Betty Ford Center was always her primary interest, and the former first lady completely immersed herself into its workings. Far from an absentee founder, she maintained a presence at the center that surprised nearly all who witnessed her dedication. John Schwarzlose, the center's president, wryly observed, "She's the boss. Her personality sets the standards and tone." One patient remembered attending an orientation at the center on the day he was admitted and finding that he was addressed by the former first lady herself. Beginning with "My name is Betty Ford, and I'm an alcoholic and an addict," she went on to explain her intervention, treatment, and recovery to the new patients in words that sound much like those used in her memoirs. As she spoke in public about the center, she found that she had to deal with the charge that the center was biased toward catering to a fabulously wealthy clientele. Mrs. Ford claimed that this was a group of patients who comprised "probably only one-tenth of 1 percent" of the total patient population at the center, and went on to explain:

> Humility is an important aspect of our program. . . . Every patient, without exception, is expected to make his or her own bed, do laundry, and take on other "therapy duty chores." The first reaction of high visibility people may be, "You mean there's no one here who can make my bed or do my laundry?" But that attitude quickly changes. . . . I've been there, so I know.[22]

Some thirty cities eventually offered to build similar centers with Betty Ford's name attached. She rejected each proposal because of her need to be personally involved with the project. She would tell her staff that she had no desire to see "Kentucky Fried Betty Fords" all over the country.[23]

Mrs. Ford's immersion in the workings of the center was only part of a newfound public advocacy, one that would make her the nation's leading spokesperson on the challenges of substance abuse and addiction for the next three decades. She chastised the insurance industry for making it difficult for patients to pay for their treatment through their insurance. In 1993 she joined the National Center on Addiction and Substance Abuse at Columbia University. Through this affiliation, she united with former Johnson cabinet member Joseph Califano and three former surgeons general to call for action against underage drinking. She also signed onto a report entitled "Under the Rug: Substance Abuse and the Mature Woman," which claimed that only 1 percent of physicians recognized the early signs of alcohol abuse in women over the age of fifty-nine—a tragedy that costs the nation some $39 billion per year.[24]

Substance abuse advocacy was not the only issue of public health that engaged Mrs. Ford. She also carved out for herself a leading role in the fight to raise funds to treat arthritis, a condition with which she is afflicted. As an honorary trustee of the National Arthritis Foundation, Mrs. Ford regularly appeared at fund-raisers, eager to dispel the myth that arthritis is, in her words, an "old person's disease." Persisting in her concern for the issue of breast cancer, she continued to promote early detection and prevention as a speaker for the Susan G. Komen Foundation in Dallas, a fund-raising group that annually gave an award named after the former first lady. She also lent her name to the Betty Ford Center for Cancer Prevention and Screening at the Grand Rapids Blodgett Memorial Medical Center.[25]

This new advocacy led to the burying of a significant political hatchet. For almost two decades, the relations between Betty Ford and Rosalynn Carter had been correct but wary. In 1984, Mrs. Ford shared the stage with Mrs. Carter, as well as several other former first ladies, first family members, and scholars, for a landmark conference on the role of the first lady, held at the Ford Library and Museum. A decade later, in 1994, they agreed to serve as honorary cochairs of the Healthcare Leadership Coalition. In early March of that year, the two former first ladies came to Washington to testify before the Senate, which had made major cuts in funding for both mental (Mrs. Carter's cause) and substance abuse treatment in the health care package being proposed by the Clinton Administration. Speaking to reporters, Mrs. Ford tried to play to the nation's pocketbook, arguing that "for every $1 spent [on treatment], $10 is returned to the economy." The next day, they testified before a committee chaired by Senator Edward Kennedy (D-MA); then they appeared on the morning talk shows, and CNN's *Larry King Live,* making the same point.[26]

This rejuvenated activism also led Mrs. Ford to write a second volume of memoirs. Published in 1987, *Betty: A Glad Awakening* centered solely on her treatment for substance abuse and the building of the Betty Ford Center. As Mrs. Ford remembered it, "The first book was on the outside—about people, places, and things. This book came very much from the inside. I thought I had examined my feelings before, but I really hadn't. I found I had carefully skipped over things. You know, honest self-deception." All proceeds from the book were donated to the Betty Ford Center and other treatment facilities.[27]

Issues of public health were, however, not Mrs. Ford's only focus during the postpresidential years. The issue of women's rights, particularly the ongoing battle for the Equal Rights Amendment, continued to be of importance to the former first lady. In 1978, the Congress agreed to extend the seven-year deadline for the ERA's passage in the states to June 30, 1982. Shortly after her stay at Long Beach, while working to raise money for what would become the Betty Ford Center, the former first lady was back on the road for the ERA, hoping to take advantage of the extension. But the tide had turned: the conservatives who had almost defeated her husband for the nomination some three years before were now gaining control of the party. In 1979, she flew to North Carolina to talk to state Republicans as they geared up for another vote. The vote never happened. In 1980, while the Democratic Party reaffirmed its traditional support for the ERA, during its platform hearings, the Republican Party reversed its forty-year record of support; the convention officially took no position on ERA in its platform. However, during the fall campaign, Ronald Reagan continued his opposition to the amendment.[28]

In 1981 Mrs. Ford was named the honorary chair of the ERA Countdown Campaign (her cochair was actor Alan Alda). The campaign organized "Countdown Rallies" in more than one hundred eighty cities to draw attention to the impending deadline for the ERA. Not surprisingly, she was no mere figurehead chairperson. In August 1981, she led 12,000 supporters of the ERA in a parade for the ERA that marched down the Avenue of the Stars in Los Angeles. Two months later, along with Lady Bird Johnson, Mrs. Ford addressed a crowd of three thousand ERA supporters from the steps of the Lincoln Memorial. Just as important, throughout 1981, she recommitted herself to her lobbying efforts of 1975 and called state legislators to argue for the passage of the

amendment. The efforts of the former first lady and the other supporters of the ERA were for naught. After Indiana ratified the
amendment in 1977, no more states ratified, even with the extension. On June 30, 1982, the ERA was stopped three states short of
ratification.[29]

Betty Ford also continued to speak out in favor of a woman's
right to choose. In 1990, along with other Republican leaders such as
Millicent Fenwick, Mary Louise Smith, and Jill Ruckelshaus, Mrs.
Ford was a founding member of PRO-CHOICE America, a political
action committee that would, according to its maiden press release,
"support courageous pro-choice Republicans who face anti-choice
opponents." She was also a member of the WISH List (Women in
the Senate and House), a group that supported prochoice female
Republican candidates.[30]

During the conservative decade of the Reagan and Bush Administrations, Mrs. Ford refused to publicly moderate her views
on abortion. This put her squarely at odds with the mainstream of
the Republican Party in the 1980s and early 1990s. As a result, an
interesting development took place, as it was Betty Ford, a former
first lady, who became the symbol for an entire wing of the
party—those who felt uncomfortable with the social engineering
that was underway by the New Right. The former first lady, who
hoped that her party would "be taking moderate stands," argued
plainly that she felt that "it has to be understood that there are ex-
tenuating circumstances where a woman must have the right to
make decisions about her own body." She was also one of the first
national celebrities to speak out against the inaction of the Reagan
and Bush administrations on AIDS, informing people that all too
often, substance abusers were HIV-positive, as was the case with
many patients at the Betty Ford Center. In 1991, she publicly
charged that within the Bush Administration's well-publicized war
on drugs, "the focus has shifted to cocaine and crack to the extent
of ignoring alcohol, the number one drug of addiction in this
country." Mrs. Ford also challenged the Bush Justice Department
when she claimed that "the regression to an addiction-as-crime
mind-set" had set the stage for insurance companies being able to
refuse payment for substance abuse treatment. Betty Ford was at
odds with the ruling wing of her own party; indeed, she was at

odds with her own husband's political and social views, although after 1980 Ford voiced them in public less and less. As Dorene Whitney, a board member of the WISH List observed, "Betty Ford is the moderate Republican."[31]

Betty Ford also continued to work her way through challenging physical pain. In November 1987, during quadruple heart bypass surgery—a procedure that received markedly little press—she had complications and, in her words, "nearly died." Indeed, within a five-month period, she needed four more surgeries. This led to a new challenge to her addictions, because she had to wean herself off the prescribed painkillers, lest she become trapped again. She remembered "there were a lot of sleepless nights when I just walked the floor . . . [but] I was able to stop." She continued to suffer from pain in her neck and shoulder; the pain could be so severe that it woke her in the middle of the night, and all she could do was sit up with a book and wait until morning. Over-the-counter painkillers to deal with an advanced stage of arthritis were useless. However, she tried a regimen of moist heat and manual traction by hospital therapists, and "when it really gets bad, ultrasound treatment." And she continued a daily fight with the disease that has become synonymous with her name, wryly observing that "the disease is alcohol*is*m, not alcohol*was*ism."[32]

The nation continued to hold Mrs. Ford dear in its affections. In 1985, she was the first recipient of AIDS Project L.A.'s Commitment to Life award. In 1987, she was inducted into the Michigan Women's History Hall of Fame. On November 18, 1991, President George H. W. Bush awarded her the Presidential Medal of Freedom, the nation's highest civilian award. In the citation, Bush read, "the nation honors a generous citizen, a creative spirit, a valiant woman who has struggled for the dignity essential for true freedom." On October 27, 1999, President Bill Clinton presented both Gerald and Betty Ford with the Congressional Gold Medal for "dedicated public service and outstanding humanitarian contributions." On January 15, 2002, she received an award from the Legal Action Center for her work in the field of substance abuse treatment. But accepting these awards, no matter how prestigious, seemed to be, at best, a necessary evil for the former first lady. After being honored in 1986 by the National Association of Alcoholism Treatment Programs, she gave an acceptance address that elicited thunderous applause: "Awards are often given to people who are old and decrepit because you don't think they'll be around much longer. Well, if that's your idea, it's premature because I don't plan to retire—and I plan to be around for quite a while."[33]

In 2002, The Betty Ford Center celebrated its twentieth anniversary. A reporter for the Palm Springs *Desert Sun* was allowed to spend five days with the women of the center's Fisher Hall and write a first-hand account of life inside the Betty Ford Center. At the end of her week, the reporter asked a series of questions of the patients she had met and lived with. Her final question: "What would you ask Betty Ford if you could ask her one question?" One patient thought a bit, and quietly said that she would just say, "Thank you."[34]

CHAPTER 7

LEGACY

How, then, to remember Betty Ford as first lady?

One must begin with her candor. This was a first lady who spoke her mind, spoke it in public, and spoke it frequently. More often than not, this frankness sent her husband's political advisers running for cover. And since she was often voicing an opinion that represented the views of the more moderate wing of the Republican Party (views often, but not always, shared by her husband), her candor enraged that portion of the populace who identified with the social goals of the growing New Right. Thus, the first lady made the task of coalition building within the moderate and conservative wings of the Republican Party more difficult for her husband, and the divisive and expensive primary battle against Ronald Reagan that arose from this inability to form a coalition was a major reason for his ultimate defeat at the hands of Jimmy Carter. And yet despite the mischief that her openness played with her husband's political ambitions, most Americans found Betty Ford's candor refreshing. In a post-Watergate world, where Americans longed to have the nylon curtain of secrecy removed from their government, Betty Ford was a breath of fresh air.

Mrs. Ford was also an active lobbyist as first lady. Yet there was less public support for her lobbying for the Equal Rights Amendment than there was for her candor in general. Also, as shown earlier, while

Mrs. Ford consistently advocated the passage of the ERA, her lobbying of Congress for the measure was of a short duration and had no
positive effect on its fate. Unlike, for example, Lady Bird Johnson,
who was instrumental in getting the Highway Beautification Act
passed through Congress, Betty Ford did not deliver the ERA. This
may have dissuaded her successors from taking an active role in lobbying for measures they supported; the next time it would be attempted—with decidedly mixed results—was by Hillary Rodham
Clinton, as she worked toward securing her husband's health re-
form proposals. Yet these conclusions should not keep us from
understanding how singular Betty Ford was in the history of presidential spouses. Up to 1974, only Eleanor Roosevelt and Lady Bird
Johnson publicly lobbied for legislative measures they supported.
And no first lady—not even Mrs. Roosevelt—has ever approached
the level of public candor that was set by Betty Ford.

However, many observers, such as scholar Robert Watson, have
taken the evidence of Mrs. Ford's lobbying and candor to an ex-
treme, claiming that she was an "active political partner of the president." Nowhere in the memoirs of either principal, nor in the available archival record, is there evidence to support such a partnership.
Gerald Ford never offered it, seems not to have desired it, and Betty
Ford never sought it. Indeed, throughout Ford's career, the story is
one of his leaving his wife to a more traditional role of homemaker
and private adviser, rather than including her in any real decision-
making processes. Although there is evidence of her giving advice to
the president on political appointments, she was clearly not his
most important adviser in this regard.[1]

Because of the closeness of their personal relationship, Betty Ford
had more success with the informal, private advocacy of the president that pundits label "pillow talk." It seems that she limited her advocacy in this regard to the realm of presidential appointments. At an
early meeting of women appointees to the administration, Ford
quipped that he had no choice but to appoint more women, because
"it's the best way to keep me out of the doghouse with Betty" (Figure
7.1). Her first coup was in Ford's choice of Carla Hills as Secretary of
Housing and Urban Development; all concerned (especially Mrs.
Ford, who mentioned it in virtually every interview on the subject)
credit the first lady's influence with swaying Ford on the appoint-

Figure 7.1. President and Mrs. Gerald R. Ford, 1986
(Russell Ohlson photograph, courtesy of Gerald R. Ford Library).

ment. She also took credit for the appointment of Anne Armstrong as ambassador to Great Britain, even though Armstrong had spent a decade in Republican politics and had served both the Nixon and Ford White Houses. Retired Air Force General Jeanne M. Holm was also named Ford's Special Assistant for Women in March 1976. According to the count of two Betty Ford scholars, thirty-six women held important positions in the Ford Administration.[2]

Yet even in this regard, Mrs. Ford was not entirely successful. She failed to convince her husband to appoint the first woman vice president in 1974. (The nod went to Nelson Rockefeller.) She also failed to get a woman Supreme Court justice (Ford nominated John Paul Stevens as an associate justice in November 1975) and a woman vice presidential candidate in 1976 (Betty lobbied for Anne Armstrong; Ford instead chose Kansas Senator Robert Dole). And although it is true that the number of female appointees increased 3 percent from the Nixon to the Ford years, it increased from a paltry 3 percent to a paltry 6 percent, despite the fact that the size of the government was quickly growing.[3]

Indeed, there are those who have looked at Mrs. Ford's attempts to affect public policy during the Ford Administration and concluded that not only did she not do so to any appreciable measure, but that she was little more than a media celebrity—the first *People* magazine first lady. Mrs. Ford herself later claimed "the media projected me as much more of an activist than I was." Some suggest that rather than be remembered in a positive vein, she should be remembered as a divisive presence that actually hurt the legacy of her husband. Yet to suggest that she may have "cost her husband . . . the historical respect his administration is now often denied" is to completely ignore the emerging positive historiography of the Ford years—a literature that suggests that he had significant domestic and foreign policy accomplishments that were hardly compromised by his wife.[4]

Such an overly harsh assessment also ignores the respect with which Betty Ford continues to be held. For the past two decades, she has been ranked near the top of almost every list that ranks first ladies. The Siena Research Institute polled more than a hundred historians and asked them to rank the forty-two first ladies (including the six cases where the first lady was not the wife of the president). In 1982, Betty Ford was ranked sixth; in 1993 she was ranked ninth. The average member of the American public seems to feel the same way; in a July 1980 poll for *Good Housekeeping*, Mrs. Ford placed sixth.[5]

This respect and affection may well come as a result of the one policy area in which Betty Ford made a seminal contribution. In the field of public advocacy for women's health issues, Mrs. Ford was a path breaker who made substantive strides toward the education of women about a disease that, at the time she was in the White House, was the number one killer of women. For all intents and purposes, Betty Ford started the breast cancer awareness movement in the United States. When assessing her fight against breast cancer, and her advocacy for early detection of the disease, a *New York Times* editorial rightfully concluded, "If Betty Ford had done nothing else as first lady, the light her trouble had shed on a dark subject would be contribution enough."[6]

She also was a seminal figure in the changing perception of substance abuse from a moral lapse to a disease. On both issues, she not only offered herself as a role model, but did so at the time that she was recovering from a disease—a rare act of courage. One measure of the success of her advocacy is in lives saved: as Zora Brown, founder and president of the Breast Cancer Resource Committee, has noted, "without Betty Ford, women would be dying in far greater numbers than they are now." Yet there is another measure: Betty Ford has become larger than life. She is the only woman in American political history—perhaps the only American politician of either sex—whose name has been transmitted to both a place and an idea, as in, "I have a problem; I am checking into Betty Ford."[7]

Indeed, it seems that the respect still held for Betty Ford is more than the sum of her public advocacy. More like Eleanor Roosevelt than any other first lady, Betty Ford has come to stand for something—a true symbol of an era, who, in the words of one scholar, "could not have been more in touch with her times." As Mrs. Roosevelt became a symbol of the battle for civil rights, Betty Ford has come to be identified by the public with those battles of the 1970s with which she was publicly involved, regardless of the depth of her role in them or her ability to make them a success. Moreover, she has become identified with a style that showed power, a "tell it like it is" woman, so trendily illustrated in a television advertisement of the time, who has "come a long way, baby." In the parlance of the day, Betty Ford was clearly an "independent woman." Although she never sought to be independent of the aura of her husband, she had an independence of spirit that led her to chart her own path in life, despite the continuing barriers placed there by the patriarchal system.[8]

Yet her candor was only a part of her legacy. Betty Ford was a woman of rare courage. This was a part of her upbringing by her mother Hortense, who was for all intents and purposes a single mother and who was a daily reminder to her daughter of strength and courage. She also learned courage as a dancer: Martha Graham would later say that "part of the training of a dancer is to meet a situation with courage and the necessity for complete honesty." But the rest, she did herself. She not only had the courage to face possible death on the operating table with grace and wit, but she refused to end her association with cancer after she was cured. Instead, she re-lived that nightmare over and over again in public so that other women might live. On the political front, rather than being afraid to face a national "character debate" about her beliefs, she seemed to seek such a debate. Indeed, she was the first first lady since Eleanor Roosevelt to be judged by the American people on the strength of her beliefs—both personal and private. And although it may have cost her, and perhaps her husband, politically, her willingness to be judged in that manner has made her a symbol of political courage. Dolores Hope did not underestimate the case when she described her friend as "a valiant woman."[9]

In her candor, courage, and grace, Betty Ford succeeded in an area where her husband tried, but ultimately failed. Gerald Ford truly wanted to restore an aura of honesty to the presidency, but the pardon doomed the effort. It was his wife who brought an atmosphere of honesty back to the White House—indeed, back to the presidency itself—after Watergate. In terms of the legacy of the Ford presidency, there is absolutely no doubt that the first lady was an asset to history. Her husband claimed that his presidency was "A Time to Heal." In her honesty and courage, Betty Ford did more to heal the wounds of Watergate than did her husband.

Three weeks before the terrorist attacks of September 11, 2001, *U.S. News and World Report* ran an eerily prescient double issue, featuring "Twenty Living American Heroes." Betty Ford was listed as one of them.[10]

After September 11, the term *hero* became a staple in news stories and reports. Although definitions of heroism were as varied as there were writers and observers, one common thread occurred in their writings—that of public courage. And yet, the heroes celebrated after September 11 were not of the caste that were celebrated in our history before that tragedy. Almost exclusively in our history, high school and college textbooks apply this definition of heroism to men, and then largely to American presidents or military men. While not questioning their inclusion, it is clear that since September 11, Americans have looked at heroism in a different light. There is, in its new definition, more of an emphasis on a less military, less public, more individual kind of courage—witness the inclusion of firemen, blood donors, and prescient post office clerks in the pantheon of post–September 11 heroes.[11]

Betty Ford is a hero of American history. In the *U.S. News and World Report* issue that rightly included her with other heroes, Betty was listed under the category of "Truth Teller." Her display of a rather singular public courage inspired men and women alike to reconsider their preconceptions about breast cancer. Her public lobbying for the ERA—itself an act of courage, despite its limited effect on the outcome of the issue—opened a discussion about the public role of the first lady that continues to the present day. And her public admission of drug and alcohol addiction, as well as her willingness to attach her name to an innovative recovery center, significantly affected American perceptions on substance abuse, as well as played a part in the shattering of medical stereotypes toward addictive diseases. As she continues to speak out on topics from AIDS to arthritis, Betty Ford continues to display those public qualities that Americans have traditionally seen as heroic.

It is entirely fitting that a patient at the Betty Ford Center should be allowed to sum up her legacy to history: "That woman is going to be long remembered—and not as the wife of a President of the United States."[12]

NOTES

DANCER

1. Betty Ford, *The Times of My Life* (New York: Harper and Row, 1978), 5–6.

2. *Chicago Today*, undated clipping, Gerald R. Ford Presidential Library, Ann Arbor, MI (GFL), clipping file.

3. Ford, *Times of My Life*, 6, 12. Betty's summer vacations at Whitefish Lake earned for her what seems to be the first photograph of her published in a newspaper—a photo of six-year-old Betty Bloomer and two of her friends, mugging for the camera at Whitefish, and printed on the front page of the local society section (*Grand Rapids Herald*, August 17, 1924).

4. Lynn Minton, "Betty Ford Talks About Her Mother," *McCall's*, May 1976, 76; *Grand Rapids Press*, February 3, 1934, and February 8, 1936.

5. Jerald F. terHorst, *Gerald Ford and the Future of the Presidency* (New York: Third Press, 1974), 193; Ford, *Times of My Life*, 9.

6. "Betty Ford: One Day at a Time," *A&E Biography* (Arts and Entertainment Television Network, 1996); James Cannon, *Time and Chance: Gerald Ford's Appointment with Destiny* (New York: Harper Collins, 1994), 46; James Cannon, interview with the author, August 12, 2002; Certificate of Death (issued July 18, 1934), Michigan Department of Health, State Office Number 14122351. Bloomer's obituary can be found in *Grand Rapids Press*, July 20, 1934, 15.

7. "Betty Ford," *A&E Biography*. For a brief but useful description of the classic enabler in an alcoholic family, see Hugh Davis Graham, "The Paradox of Eleanor Roosevelt: Alcoholism's Child," *Virginia Quarterly Review* 63 (spring 1987): 223–24; *Los Angeles Times*, November 12, 1995; Betty Ford, *Betty: A Glad Awakening* (Garden City, NY: Doubleday, 1987), 32; Oriana Jossean Kalant, *Alcohol and Drug Problems in Women: Research Advances in Alcohol and Drug Problems*, vol. 5 (New York: Plenum, 1980), 299–300. A good primer for this issue is "The Genetics of Alcoholism," at the "What You Need to Know About Alcoholism" Web site, at http://alcoholism.about.com/library/blnaa18.htm. See also N. S. Cotton, "The Familial Incidence of Alcoholism: A Review," *Journal of Studies on Alcohol* 40 (1979): 89–116.

8. "Betty Ford," *A&E Biography*; Ford, *Times of My Life*, 7; Minton, "Betty Ford Talks About Her Mother," 74, 76.

9. Minton, "Betty Ford Talks About Her Mother," 76; Myra MacPherson, "Betty Ford at 60: 'My Life is Just Beginning,'" *McCall's*, March 1979, 139.

10. Minton, "Betty Ford Talks About Her Mother," 78.

11. Ford, *Times of My Life*, 16.

12. Martha Graham, *Blood Memory* (New York: Doubleday, 1991), 5; Ford, *Times of My Life*, 13, 17; "Betty Ford," *A&E Biography*; Jeffrey Ashley, *Betty Ford: A Symbol of Strength* (New York: Nova History Publications, 2003), 12; undated clipping, GFL; Molly Schaefer, "When Betty Ford Was the Pavlova of Grand Rapids," *People Weekly*, November 18, 1974, 55–58.

13. Ford, *Times of My Life*, 17; Marian Horosko, comp., *Martha Graham: The Evolution of Her Dance Theory and Training* (Chicago: a cappella books, 1991), 2, 43.

14. Quoted in terHorst, *Gerald Ford*, 195; Ford, *Times of My Life*, 23.

15. See Graham, *Blood Memory*, 162 and passim; Horosko, *Martha Graham*, 1, 18.

16. Jean Liebman Block, "The Betty Ford Nobody Knows," *Good Housekeeping*, May 1974, 139.

17. *Greensboro Daily News*, May 23, 1976; Block, "Betty Ford Nobody Knows," 139; Ford, *Times of My Life*, 24. On October 14, 1976, Graham, then eighty-two years old, was awarded a Presidential Medal of Freedom by then President Gerald R. Ford—the first such award given to a dancer or a choreographer. Of the award, Graham would later write, "this marked me, as the Japanese mark their artists, as a national treasure" (*Blood Memory*, 169).

18. Ford, *Times of My Life*, 26, 29, 31; *New York Times*, June 20, 1975; Horosko, *Martha Graham*, 168; Block, "Betty Ford Nobody Knows," 139; Fact Sheet, "Betty Ford and Martha Graham: Background," undated (1975), Betty Ford Papers, GFL, Trip File, box 10, New York City—Martha Graham, folder 1.

19. Ashley, *Betty Ford*, 19; Ford, *Times of My Life*, 31–32.

20. Mrs. Collins C. Clark, interview, Grand Rapids Oral History Collection, GFL, 2; Ford, *Times of My Life*, 33; MacPherson, "Betty Ford at 60," 139.

21. Bill Bloomer, in "Betty Ford," *A&E Biography*; Ford, *Times of My Life*, 34, 36–37.

22. Ashley, *Betty Ford*, 20.

23. Ford, *Times of My Life*, 14, 37; divorce record (issued December 15, 1947), Michigan Department of Health, State Office Number 4114726; Ford, *Times of My Life*, 38.

24. Ford, *Times of My Life*, 39, 40; *Grand Rapids Press*, August 11, 1943; May 2, 1946, and November 27, 1946; *Grand Rapids Herald*, November 27, 1946; *Toledo Blade*, August 10, 1974; Clark interview, GFL, 3.

25. Ford, *Times of My Life*, 36, 41; Kalant, *Alcohol and Drug Problems*, 301.

26. Ford, *Times of My Life*, 41–43; Cannon, *Time and Chance*, 47.

27. Divorce record (issued December 15, 1947), Michigan Department of Health, State Office Number 4114726; Ford, *Times of My Life*, 43. For his part, Warren moved to the West Coast, settled in the San Francisco area, and remarried. See *San Francisco Chronicle*, undated clipping, White House Social Files, Subject Files, GFL, box 23, folder 13.

28. Ford, *Times of My Life*, 43.

"THE CONGRESS GOT A MINORITY LEADER, AND I LOST A HUSBAND"

1. "Betty Ford: One Day at a Time," *A&E Biography* (Arts and Entertainment Television Network, 1996); Gerald R. Ford, *A Time to Heal* (New York: Harper and Row, 1979), 42–61; James Cannon, *Time and Chance: Gerald Ford's Appointment with Destiny* (New York: Harper Collins, 1994), 1–39; John Robert Greene, *The Presidency of Gerald R. Ford* (Lawrence: University Press of Kansas, 1995), 1–3.

2. Ford, *Time to Heal*, 62–63; Cannon, *Time and Chance*, 42–43.

3. "Betty Ford," *A&E Biography*; Betty Ford, *The Times of My Life* (New York: Harper and Row, 1978), 47. James Cannon, interview with the author, August 12, 2002; Barbara Howar, "Spotlight on Betty Ford: A New Breed of Wife in the Nation's Capital," *Family Circle*, November 1974, 141.

4. Ford, *Time to Heal*, 64; Cannon, *Time and Chance*, 51; Jerald F. terHorst, *Gerald Ford and the Future of the Presidency* (New York: Third Press, 1974), 24.

5. Ford, *Times of My Life*, 54–55; Ford, *Time to Heal*, 65; "Betty Ford," *A&E Biography*.

6. Bud Vestal, *Jerry Ford Up Close: An Investigative Biography* (New York: Coward, McCann, and Geoghegan, 1974), 94–95; Ford, *Times of My Life*, 54, 58–61; Ford, *Time to Heal*, 67; "Betty Ford," *A&E Biography*.

7. Ford, *Times of My Life*, ix, 55.

8. For more information, see the Ancestry.com Web site, at http://awt.ancestry.com/cgi-bin/igm.cgi?op=GET&db=rum1800&id=I23488. Hortense's obituary can be found at *Grand Rapids Press*, November 23, 1948.

9. Greene, *Presidency of Ford*, 3–4.

10. Ibid., 4–6.

11. Ford, *Times of My Life*, 62–65; quoted in Cannon, *Time and Chance*, 56.

12. Jane Howard, "Forward Day by Day," *New York Times Magazine*, December 4, 1974, 64; Ford, *Time to Heal*, 15; Cannon interview with author.

13. Jean Liebman Block, "The Betty Ford Nobody Knows," *Good Housekeeping*, May 1974, 140; Gloria Steinem, "Betty Ford Today: Still Speaking Out," *Ms.*, April 1984, 41.

14. Steinem, "Betty Ford Today," 41.

15. John Robert Greene, *Gerald R. Ford: A Bibliography* (Westport, CT: Greenwood Press, 1974), 123. Throughout this period, to maintain residence in Michigan, the Fords also kept an apartment in Grand Rapids—it was half of a two-family house, and the other half was rented out.

16. Ford, *Time to Heal*, 71; Vestal, *Jerry Ford Up Close*, 128.

17. Jack Ford, interview with the author, April 17, 2003; "The Relentless Ordeal of Political Wives," *Time*, October 7, 1974, 20; Ford, *Times of My Life*, 10, 90.

18. Ford, *Times of My Life*, 10; Block, "Betty Ford Nobody Knows," 140; Cannon, *Time and Chance*, 79.

19. Ford, *Times of My Life*, 120; Ford, *Time to Heal*, 71.

20. Trude B. Feldman, "The Closest Family in Washington," *McCall's*, May 1974, 140; Block, "Betty Ford Nobody Knows," 141; Phyllis Battelle, "Betty Ford Battles Arthritis—Every Day," *50-Plus*, January 1985, 47; Ford, *Times of My Life*, 117–18; Ford, *Time to Heal*, 83; Cannon, *Time and Chance*, 78.

21. Betty Friedan, *The Feminine Mystique* (New York: Dell, 1977), 10, 27.

22. Betty Ford, *Betty: A Glad Awakening* (Garden City, NY: Doubleday, 1987), 33, 36; Steinem, "Betty Ford Today," 42; Ford, *Times of My Life*, 124–25; Cannon, *Time and Chance*, 74.

23. "Betty Ford," *A&E Biography*; Block, "Betty Ford Nobody Knows," 141; Ford, *Times of My Life*, 123–24; Cannon, *Time and Chance*, 88; quoted in Myra G. Gutin and Leesa E. Tobin, "'You've Come a Long Way, Mr. President': Betty Ford as First Lady," in Bernard J. Firestone and Alexej Ugrinsky, eds., *Gerald R. Ford and the Politics of Post-Watergate America*, vol. 2 (Westport, CT: Greenwood Press, 1993), 625; Ford, *Glad Awakening*, 36.

24. "Betty Ford," *A&E Biography*; Ford, *Time to Heal*, 99, 294; Bruce Cassiday, *Betty Ford: Woman of Courage* (New York: Dale Books, 1978), 50.

25. John Robert Greene, *The Limits of Power: The Nixon and Ford Administrations* (Bloomington: Indiana University Press, 1992), 167–68, 186–87.

26. Stephen Ambrose, *Nixon: Ruin and Recovery, 1973–1990* (New York: Simon and Schuster, 1991), 236–37.

27. Ford, *Time to Heal*, 105–7; Ambrose, *Nixon*, 238; Saul Friedman, "In Praise of Honest Ignorance: A Kind Word for Jerry Ford," *Harper's*, August 1974, 20; Block, "Betty Ford Nobody Knows," 142.

28. Richard M. Nixon, *Public Papers of the President, 1973* (Washington, DC: U.S. Government Printing Office, 1973), 867–69; Ambrose, *Nixon*, 238–39; Lester A. Sobel, ed., *Presidential Succession: Ford, Rockefeller and the 25th Amendment* (New York: Facts on File, 1975), 42.

29. Ford, *Times of My Life*, 147; Robert T. Hartmann, *Palace Politics: An Inside Account of the Ford Years* (New York: McGraw-Hill, 1980), 27.

30. Dom Bonafede, "White House Report: Ford and Staff: Tend to Business . . . and Wait," *National Journal Reports*, August 10, 1974, 1179; "The President Should Resign," *Time*, November 12, 1973, 19.

31. Ford, *Time to Heal*, 109; Joel Goldstein, *The Modern American Vice Presidency: The Transformation of a Political Institution* (Princeton, NJ: Princeton University Press, 1982), 242.

32. Undated memo, Benton Becker Papers, Gerald R. Ford Presidential Library, Ann Arbor, MI (GFL), box 1, Winter-Burger folder; Cannon, *Time and Chance*, 240–42.

33. Hartmann, *Palace Politics*, 87; *Vital Speeches*, December 15, 1973, 149.

34. "Betty Ford," *A&E Biography;* Cannon, interview with the author; Howard, "Forward Day by Day," 40; Greene, *Presidency of Ford*, 13.

35. Block, "Betty Ford Nobody Knows," 138.

36. Feldman, "Closest Family in Washington," 94.

37. "Betty Ford," *A&E Biography;* Myra Gutin, *The President's Partner: The First Lady in the Twentieth Century* (Westport, CT: Greenwood Press, 1989), 138.

38. Cannon, interview with the author; quoted in Trude B. Feldman, "New First Lady," *McCall's*, October 1974, 88; terHorst, *Gerald Ford*, 201. Jane Howard, "Forward Day by Day," *New York Times Magazine*, December 4, 1974, 36.

39. Gutin, *President's Partner*, 131; Ford, *Times of My Life*, 152, 154; Hartmann, *Palace Politics*, 121; terHorst, *Gerald Ford*, 202–3; speech notes, June 8, 1974, in Gerald R. Ford Vice Presidential Papers, GFL, Speech File, box 134, dated folder (emphasis in text).

40. Feldman, "Closest Family in Washington," 138; Block, "Betty Ford Nobody Knows," 142; Howard, "Forward Day by Day," 40; Howar, "Spotlight on Betty Ford," 140.

41. Notes, August 8, 1974, from *Newsweek* Magazine Copy, Center for American History, University of Texas, Austin.

42. Ford, *Glad Awakening*, 38; Cannon, *Time and Chance*, 74.

43. Rosalynn Carter, *First Lady from Plains* (Boston: Houghton Mifflin, 1984), 99–100; Carl Sferrazza Anthony, *First Ladies: The Saga of the Presidents' Wives and Their Power*, vol. 2 (New York: William Morrow, 1991), 209.

44. *Grand Rapids Press*, October 13, 1974; *Washington Star*, November 11, 1973; Ford, *Times of My Life*, 150; Vestal, *Jerry Ford Up Close*, 179; Peter Hay, *All the Presidents' Ladies: Anecdotes of Women Behind the Men in the White House* (New York: Viking, 1988), 252.

45. Howar, "Spotlight on Betty Ford," 97.

46. Clifton Daniel, *Lords, Ladies, and Gentlemen: A Memoir* (New York: Arbor House, 1984), 126.

47. Greene, *Presidency of Ford*, 13–15.

48. Anthony, *First Ladies*, 217; *New York Times*, August 9, 1974; Ford, *Times of My Life*, 3; Ford, *Time to Heal*, 39.

49. terHorst, *Gerald Ford*, 169; Ford, *Times of My Life*, 4; ABC News special, *A New Presidency*, tape 3, August 9, 1974, GFL, Audio-Visual, video F27; Ford, *Time to Heal*, 33, 38; Anthony, *First Ladies*, 220.

50. "Elizabeth (Anne Bloomer) Ford," *Current Biography* (New York: H. W. Wilson, September 1975), 21; Ford, *Times of My Life*, 1.

"SHE WAS BEGINNING TO FLOWER A LITTLE"

1. *Newsweek Magazine* Copy, Center for American History, University of Texas, Austin; Betty Ford, *The Times of My Life* (New York: Harper and Row, 1978), 162, 164; quoted in Hugh Sidey and Fred Ward, *Portrait of a President* (New York: Harper and Row, 1975), 36; *New York Times*, August 18, 1974.

2. *Washington Post*, April 28, 1991; John Robert Greene, *The Presidency of Gerald R. Ford* (Lawrence: University Press of Kansas, 1995), 21–25; See Parker to Jones, August 15, 1974, Robert T. Hartmann Files, Gerald R. Ford Presidential Library, Ann Arbor, MI (GFL), box 170, White House Staff Organization: First Lady folder.

3. *Washington Post*, August 24, 1974.

4. Carl Sferrazza Anthony, *First Ladies: The Saga of the Presidents' Wives and Their Power*, vol. 2 (New York: William Morrow, 1991), 227; Jerald F. terHorst, *Gerald Ford and the Future of the Presidency* (New York: Third Press, 1974), 200; *New York Post*, August 31, 1974.

5. Greene, *Presidency of Ford*, 25–28, 64–66, 161–62.

6. Myra MacPherson, *The Power Lovers: An Intimate Look at Politics and Marriage* (New York: Putnam, 1975), 151; Richard Reeves, *A Ford, Not A Lincoln* (New York: Harcourt Brace Jovanovich, 1975), 48; Robert T. Hartmann, *Palace*

Politics: An Inside Account of the Ford Years (New York: McGraw-Hill, 1980), 190–91; Sheila Raab Weidenfeld, *First Lady's Lady: With the Fords at the White House* (New York: Putnam, 1979), 61; Gerald R. Ford, *A Time to Heal* (New York: Harper and Row, 1979), 187.

7. Parker to Jones, August 15, 1974, Robert T. Hartmann Papers, GFL, box 170, White House Staff Organization—First Lady folder; Betty Houchin Winfield, "Madame President: Understanding a New Kind of First Lady," *Media Studies Journal* 8 (1994): 62; Anthony, *First Ladies,* 223; "Elizabeth (Anne Bloomer) Ford," *Current Biography* (New York: H. W. Wilson, September 1975), 22; *New York Times,* August 14, 1974; Ford, *Times of My Life,* 208–9; Weidenfeld, *First Lady's Lady,* 29–30.

8. "Betty: The New First Lady," *Newsweek,* August 19, 1974, 30; John Osborne, *White House Watch: The Ford Years* (Washington, DC: New Republic Books, 1977), 178; Anthony, *First Ladies,* 226.

9. *New York Times,* September 5, 1974. A transcript of the press conference can be found in Ron Nessen Files, GFL, Subject File, box 40, Material Not Released to the Press: First Lady's Press Conference folder.

10. *Washington Post,* September 6, 1974.

11. Sidey and Ward, *Portrait,* 77; Greene, *Presidency of Ford,* 53–60.

12. Anthony, *First Ladies,* 234; *New York Times,* September 9, 1974; Helen Thomas, *Thanks for the Memories, Mr. President* (New York: Scribner, 2002), 101; Margaret Truman, *First Ladies* (New York: Random House, 1995), 134; Ford, *Times of My Life,* 181.

13. Ford, *Times of My Life,* 182; Weidenfeld, *First Lady's Lady,* 8.

14. Ford, *Time to Heal,* 190; Ford, *Times of My Life,* 182–83.

15. Ford, *Times of My Life,* 183–84; Ford, *Time to Heal,* 190.

16. Ford, *Times of My Life,* 184; Ford, *Time to Heal,* 191.

17. Ford, *Times of My Life,* 184; September 28, 1974, press conference; Ford, *Time to Heal,* 190–91. *New York Times,* September 28, 1974, September 29, 1974, September 30, 1974, October 1, 1974; Ron Nessen, *It Sure Looks Different from the Inside* (Chicago: Playboy Press, 1978), 20.

18. Quoted in Sidey and Ward, *Portrait,* 125; "Betty Ford's Operation," *Newsweek,* October 7, 1974, 30–33; transcript of press conference, September 28, 1974, Ron Nessen Papers, GFL, Subject File, box 11, Ford, Betty—Hospitalization folder; *Washington Star,* November 17, 1974; Nessen, *It Sure Looks Different,* 21.

19. Ford, *Times of My Life,* 183; Lucy Winchester to Ford, October 1, 1975, Presidential Handwriting File, GFL, box 39, President—Personal, Family folder; Ford, *Time to Heal,* 191; Hartmann, *Palace Politics,* 294; Nessen, *It Sure Looks Different,* 20; Ford, *Times of My Life,* 185.

20. Hartmann, *Palace Politics*, 295; Ford, *Time to Heal*, 193.

21. Marba Perrott to Mrs. W. J. Martin, November 7, 1974, White House Social File, Subject Files, GFL, box 193, White House Administration. For examples of letters to Betty, see White House Social File, Subject Files, GFL, FL 13-8, boxes 24–29; news summary, September 27, 1974, Sheila Weidenfeld Files, GFL, box 2, Breast Surgery folder no. 1; Betty Rollin, *First, You Cry* (New York: Lippincott, 1976), 7.

22. *Washington Star*, October 1, 1974.

23. Exhibit, Gerald R. Ford Presidential Museum, Grand Rapids, MI; Oliver Cope, MD, "New Hope for Treatment of Breast Cancer to Avoid the Surgery All Women Fear," *Vogue*, October 15, 1970, 82+; "Early Warning System," *Time*, December 27, 1971, 41; Albert Q. Maisel, "Controversy Over Breast Cancer," *Reader's Digest*, December 1971, 151–56; *New York Times*, October 1, 1974, November 12, 1972, January 14, 1975, January 25, 1976, November 7, 1976; Betty Rollin, *First, You Cry*, 18; "What Women Don't Know About Breast Cancer," *Consumer Reports*, March 1974, 264.

24. In 1974, Ford named Temple Black Ambassador to Ghana; in 1976, he named her the nation's first female chief of protocol.

25. James Cannon, *Time and Chance: Gerald Ford's Appointment with Destiny* (New York: Harper Collins, 1994), 1–2; Lester David, "A Brave Family Faces Up to Breast Cancer," *Today's Health*, June 1972, 16+.

26. Ford, *Times of My Life*, 186; transcript of press conference, September 27, 1974, Nessen Papers, GFL, Press Secretary's Press Briefings, box 2, dated folder; Nessen, *It Sure Looks Different*, 22; Gloria Steinem, "Betty Ford Today: Still Speaking Out," *Ms.*, April 1984, 42; Kathryn Casey, "We Are Survivors," *Ladies Home Journal*, September 1991, 172.

27. Myra Gutin, *The President's Partner: The First Lady in the Twentieth Century* (Westport, CT: Greenwood Press, 1989), 135; speech, American Cancer Society, November 7, 1975, Kaye Pullen Papers, GFL, box 3 (also at Gerald R. Ford Library Web site, at http://128.83.78.237/library/bbfspeeches/751107.htm).

28. Anthony, *First Ladies*, 230–31; *New York Times*, December 2, 1976.

29. Weidenfeld to Betty Ford, December 4, 1974, Weidenfeld Files, GFL, Administrative Subject File, box 49, East Wing: Press Office Organization folder; Jack Ford, interview with the author, April 17, 2003.

30. Hoopes to Connor, July 9, 1975, David Hoopes Files, Subject Files, GFL, First Lady's Office, General, folder 2.

31. See Sarah Hunter Graham, *Woman Suffrage and the New Democracy* (New Haven, CT: Yale University Press, 1996), esp. 107–27.

32. Aileen Kraditor, *The Ideas of the Women's Suffrage Movement, 1870–1920* (New York: Norton, 1980), passim; Hunter Graham, *Woman Suffrage,* esp. chap. 6; quoted in Joan Hoff-Wilson, ed., *Rights of Passage: The Past and Future of the ERA* (Bloomington: Indiana University Press, 1986), 121.

33. Jane J. Mansbridge, *Why We Lost the ERA* (Chicago: University of Chicago Press, 1986), 8.

34. Susan Hartmann, *The Home Front and Beyond: American Women in the 1940's* (Boston: Twayne, 1982), esp. 130–32; Leila J. Rupp and Verta Taylor, *Survival in the Doldrums: The American Women's Rights Movement, 1945 to the 1960's* (New York: Oxford University Press, 1987), 26–27, 59–64, 130–31; Robert H. Ferrell, ed., *Off the Record: The Private Papers of Harry S. Truman* (New York: Harper and Row, 1980), 68; Gil Troy, *Mr. and Mrs. President: From the Trumans to the Clintons,* 2nd ed. (Lawrence: University Press of Kansas, 2000), 80.

35. Sara Evans, *Tidal Wave: How Women Changed America at Century's End* (New York: Free Press, 2003), 5–6.

36. Evans, *Tidal Wave,* 21–22; Mansbridge, *Why We Lost the ERA,* 10; Donald G. Mathews and Jane Sherron De Hart, *Sex, Gender, and the Politics of ERA: A State and the Nation* (New York: Oxford University Press, 1990), 31–33.

37. "The Redstocking Manifesto," quoted in Marcia Cohen, *The Sisterhood: The True Story of the Women Who Changed the World* (New York: Simon and Schuster, 1988), 169; Evans, *Tidal Wave, 47;* Shulamith Firestone, *The Dialectic of Sex: The Case for Feminist Revolution* (New York: William Morrow, 1970), 233.

38. Evans, *Tidal Wave,* 63.

39. Mansbridge, *Why We Lost the ERA,* 10.

40. Mathews and De Hart, *Sex, Gender,* 28, 35–40. Since 1919, Congress had placed a seven-year deadline on every amendment, with the exception of the Nineteenth Amendment.

41. Mansbridge, *Why We Lost the ERA,* 12.

42. For background on Schlafly, see the Conservative Chronicle Web site, at http://conservativechronicle.com/columnists/schlafly.htm; and the biographies at the "Distinguished Women of Past and Present" Web site, at http://www .distinguishedwomen.com/biographies/schlafly.html.

43. Putney and Putney to "Legislator," March 22, 1974, Bruce A. Smathers Papers, Florida Department of State at the Florida Bureau of Archives and Records Management Web site, at http://www.floridamemory.com/Florida Highlights/ERA/ERA.cfm; Hoff-Wilson, *Rights of Passage,* 85; quoted in Riane T. Eisler, *The Equal Rights Handbook* (Lincoln, NE: iUniverse, 1998), 133–34; Mansbridge, *Why We Lost the ERA,* 223n.

44. Mathews and De Hart, *Sex, Gender,* 50–51, 270; Betty Boyd Caroli, *First Ladies* (New York: Oxford University Press, 1987), 259; Myra G. Gutin and Leesa E. Tobin, "'You've Come a Long Way, Mr. President': Betty Ford as First Lady," in Bernard J. Firestone and Alexej Ugrinsky, eds., *Gerald R. Ford and the Politics of Post-Watergate America,* vol. 2 (Westport, CT: Greenwood Press, 1993), 628.

45. Greene, *Presidency of Ford,* 4–5; John Robert Greene, *The Limits of Power: The Nixon and Ford Administrations* (Bloomington: Indiana University Press, 1992), 20, 208–9.

46. Joan Hoff, *Nixon Reconsidered* (New York: Basic Books, 1994), 105–9; Flora Davis, *Moving the Mountain: The Women's Movement in America Since 1960* (Bloomington: University of Illinois Press, 1999), 125; *Washington Star,* April 15, 1975; question-and-answer session with students at Stanford University School of Law, September 21, 1975, Gerald R. Ford, *Public Papers of the President: 1976,* vol. 1 (Washington, DC: U.S. Government Printing Office, 1980), 1482.

47. Sherry Angel, "This Ford Has a Future," *60-Plus,* September 1986, 26; Ford, *Times of My Life,* 203; Jack Ford, interview with the author; Barbara Howar, "Spotlight on Betty Ford: A New Breed of Wife in the Nation's Capital," *Family Circle,* November 1974, 141.

48. Betty Ford to Missouri Home Economics Association, April 23, 1976, Elizabeth O'Neill Files, GFL, box 2, ERA folder (emphasis added).

49. Meeting notes, October 1974, Weidenfeld Files, GFL, Administrative Subject Files, box 51, Meeting, October 1974, Liz Carpenter folder. For background on Lady Bird Johnson's efforts toward passage of the Highway Beautification Act, see Lewis L. Gould, *Lady Bird Johnson: Our Environmental First Lady* (Lawrence: University Press of Kansas, 1999), chap. 5.

50. Jules Witcover, *Marathon: The Pursuit of the Presidency, 1972–1976* (New York: Viking, 1977), 533; Weidenfeld, *First Lady's Lady,* 68–69.

51. Letter format (undated), Weidenfeld Files, GFL, General Subject Files, box 37, Ford, Betty: ERA folder; Weidenfeld, *First Lady's Lady,* 68–72; Gutin and Tobin, "You've Come a Long Way," 627; Jan Czarnik to Weidenfeld, February 7, 1975, Weidenfeld Files, GFL, General Subject Files, box 47, Women—ERA folder.

52. Myra MacPherson, "The Blooming of Betty Ford," *McCall's,* September 1975, 124.

53. Weidenfeld, *First Lady's Lady,* 74.

54. *New York Times,* February 8, 1975; Weidenfeld, *First Lady's Lady,* 78.

55. Quoted in Sherry M. La Fiette, "Betty Ford and the Equal Rights Amendment," unpublished essay, University of Texas, Austin, 12; Betty Ford to

James Washburn, March 20, 1975, Weidenfeld Files, GFL, General Subject Files, box 47, Women—ERA folder; Weidenfeld, *First Lady's Lady*, 113.

56. "A Talk with Betty," *Newsweek*, December 29, 1975, 22.

"I JUST FIGURED THAT IT WAS
TIME THAT SOMEBODY SPOKE UP"

1. *New York Times*, February 21, 1975; Kay Rohrer, "'If There Was Anything You Forgot to Ask': The Papers of Betty Ford," in Nancy Kegan Smith and Mary C. Ryan, eds., *Modern First Ladies: Their Documentary Legacy* (Washington, DC: National Archives and Records Administration, 1989), 139; letters in White House Social File, Subject Files, Gerald R. Ford Presidential Library, Ann Arbor, MI (GFL), FL-2, box 12; Myra MacPherson, "The Blooming of Betty Ford," *McCall's*, September 1975, 122; *New York Times*, February 8, 1975; Myra G. Gutin and Leesa E. Tobin, "'You've Come a Long Way, Mr. President': Betty Ford as First Lady," in Bernard J. Firestone and Alexej Ugrinsky, eds., *Gerald R. Ford and the Politics of Post-Watergate America*, vol. 2 (Westport, CT: Greenwood Press, 1993), 628.

2. Phyllis Schlafly to Betty Ford, February 8, 1975, Sheila Weidenfeld Files, General Subject Files, GFL, box 47, Women—ERA folder; MacPherson, "Blooming of Betty Ford," 120.

3. Buchen to Howe, Perrot, Ruwe, and Weidenfeld, March 4, 1975, Philip Buchen Files, GFL, box 49, Betty Ford folder no. 1.

4. Talking Points, Weidenfeld Files, General Subject Files, GFL, box 47, Women-ERA folder (emphasis in original).

5. *New York Times*, February 24, 1975; Sharon Z. Alter, "First Ladies as Activists and Leaders in the Contemporary Presidency: Betty Ford to Hillary Rodham Clinton," paper prepared for delivery at the 1998 Meeting of the Midwest Political Science Association (GFL, Uncatalogued Papers), 6.

6. Rosalynn Carter, *First Lady from Plains* (Boston: Houghton Mifflin, 1984), 99–100; Carl Sferrazza Anthony, *First Ladies: The Saga of the Presidents' Wives and Their Power*, vol. 2 (New York: William Morrow, 1991), 209, 225; Sheila Raab Weidenfeld, *First Lady's Lady: With the Fords at the White House* (New York: Putnam, 1979), 224; MacPherson, "Blooming of Betty Ford," 122.

7. Betty Ford, *The Times of My Life* (New York: Harper and Row, 1978), 280; Betty Ford, *Betty: A Glad Awakening* (Garden City, NY: Doubleday, 1987), 38; Betty Ford, "The Best Years of My Life," *McCall's*, May 1993, 92; Ron Nessen, *It Sure Looks Different from the Inside* (Chicago: Playboy Press, 1978), 23.

8. Ford, *Times of My Life*, 234.

9. Jerry Jones to David Hoopes, January 14, 1975; David Hoopes to Robert Linder, January 14, 1975, David Hoopes Files, GFL, Subject File, First Lady's Office—Personnel/Personnel Actions folder 1; Frances Spatz Leighton, "New Job at the White House: Betty Ford's Best Friend," *Family Weekly*, March 2, 1975, 29; Weidenfeld, *First Lady's Lady*, 84–85.

10. Weidenfeld, *First Lady's Lady*, 108; Ford, *Times of My Life*, 180.

11. Maxine Cheshire, *Maxine Cheshire: Reporter* (Boston: Houghton Mifflin, 1978), 214. Howe's participation in the cocktail hour was also noticed by reporter Betty Beale, and noted in *Washington Star*, October 6, 1974.

12. *Daily News (New York)*, April 12, 1975; Walter Scott, "Personality Parade," *Parade*, June 8, 1975, 1.

13. Cheshire, *Maxine Cheshire*, 204; Weidenfeld, *First Lady's Lady*, 100.

14. Cheshire, *Maxine Cheshire*, 220; *Washington Post*, April 12, 1975; Weidenfeld, *First Lady's Lady*, 98–104; Talking Points, April 11, 1975, Ron Nessen Papers, GFL, Subject File, box 11, Ford, Betty—General folder.

15. *Washington Post*, April 12, 1975; Cheshire, *Maxine Cheshire*, 221.

16. Weidenfeld, *First Lady's Lady*, 108; Ford, *Times of My Life*, 234–35.

17. Ford, *Times of My Life*, 235; *Washington Star*, April 12, 1975.

18. Ford, *Times of My Life*, 235 (those agreeing with this explanation for Howe's termination, or reporting it unchallenged, include Anthony, *First Ladies*, 248; and Nessen, *It Sure Looks Different*, 27); *Washington Post*, April 11, 1975; Partial Transcript, Nessen Briefing, April 11, 1975, Nessen Papers, GFL, Subject File, box 11, Ford, Betty—General; Cheshire, *Maxine Cheshire*, 214.

19. Ford, *Times of My Life*, 235; Cheshire, *Maxine Cheshire*, 224; Buchen to Milanowski, April 28, 1975, and memo to Buchen, undated, Buchen Files, GFL, box 42, Personnel—White House, Howe, Nancy folder.

20. Handwritten notes, Weidenfeld Files, Subject Files, GFL, box 50, East Wing Staff: Ruwe, Nancy folder; Weidenfeld, *First Lady's Lady*, 156–57; Maria Downs, "Mostly Wine and Roses," unpublished manuscript, Maria Downs Papers, GFL, box 1, 16–17; *Chicago Tribune*, November 22, 1975.

21. Gerald R. Ford, *Public Papers of the President, 1975*, vol. 1 (Washington: DC: U.S. Government Printing Office, 1978), 25; *New York Times*, January 10, 1975; Ford, *Times of My Life*, 166; Myra Gutin, *The President's Partner: The First Lady in the Twentieth Century* (Westport, CT: Greenwood Press, 1989), 142; Gutin and Tobin, "You've Come a Long Way," 627.

22. *Washington Star*, April 15, 1975; Alter, "First Ladies as Activists," 9; Davis to Scowcroft, June 12, 1975, handwritten notes (undated), Weidenfeld Files, GFL, box 47, International Women's Year Conference folder.

23. Gloria Steinem, "Betty Ford Today: Still Speaking Out," *Ms.*, April 1984, 42.

24. Weidenfeld, *First Lady's Lady*, 89; Suzanne St. Pierre to Don Hewitt and Morley Safer, July 2, 1975, Weidenfeld Files, GFL, box 37, Ford, Betty: Biography folder.

25. Frank Coffey, *60 Minutes: 25 Years of Television's Finest Hour* (Los Angeles: General Publishing Group, 1993), 209–10; transcript, *60 Minutes*, Sunday, August 10, 1975, in vertical file (Betty Ford, 1975), at GFL. "Woman of the Year," *Newsweek*, December 29, 1975, 19; Jeffrey Feinman, *Betty Ford* (New York: Award Books, 1976), chap. 1; Eliot Fremont Smith, "Reporting (Gasp!) What Betty Ford Said," *Columbia Journalism Review* 14 (November–December 1975): 15–17; Weidenfeld, *First Lady's Lady*, 148–49.

26. Coffey, *60 Minutes*, 75.

27. Feinman, *Betty Ford*, 7–18; "Betty Ford: One Day at a Time," *A&E Biography* (Arts and Entertainment Television Network, 1996).

28. Gil Troy, *Mr. and Mrs. President: From the Trumans to the Clintons*, 2nd ed. (Lawrence: University Press of Kansas, 2000), 220; Weidenfeld, *First Lady's Lady*, 158.

29. Coffey, *60 Minutes*, 75; Pamela Warrick, "Living Out Loud," *Los Angeles Times*, November 12, 1995, E2; Ford, *Times of My Life*, 206; "Betty Ford: One Day at a Time," *A&E Biography;* Perrott to Betty Ford, August 15, 1975, Elizabeth O'Neill Files, GFL, box 1, Columbia Broadcasting System folder.

30. *Manchester Union-Leader*, August 13, 1975; *New York Times*, August 21, 1975; Weidenfeld, *First Lady's Lady*, 163; *Daily News (New York)*, April 14, 1976; *Washington Post*, April 28, 1991.

31. Lloyd Shearer, "Sheila Weidenfeld: The First Lady's Press Secretary," *Parade*, April 25, 1976, 2; Angell to Weidenfeld, April 30, 1976, White House Social File, GFL, Subject File, box 12, FL-2 folder.

32. Weidenfeld, *First Lady's Lady*, 161; transcript of interview, January 2, 1977, Ron Nessen Files, GFL, presidential media interviews, box 33, dated folder; Margaret Truman, *First Ladies* (New York: Random House, 1995), 138; Nessen to Cheney, August 26, 1975, Nessen Papers, GFL, White House Memoranda File, box 127, Cheney folder; interview with television reporters; Gerald R. Ford, *Public Papers of the President, 1975*, vol. 2 (Washington, DC: U.S. Government Printing Office, 1978), 1222.

33. John Osborne, *White House Watch: The Ford Years* (Washington, DC: New Republic Books, 1977), 178; undated clip, Philip Buchen Files, GFL, box 49, President—Personal: Family, Betty Ford folder.

34. Ford, *Time to Heal*, 295.

35. Ford, *Time to Heal*, 309–10; David Hume Kennerly, *Shooter* (New York: Newsweek Books, 1979), 188–89; Ford, *Times of My Life*, 236; Reflections of President Gerald R. Ford, September 5, 1975, Buchen Files: Subject, GFL, box 43, Assassination Attempt—Fromme folder; *New York Times*, September 6, 1975.

36. Nessen, *It Sure Looks Different*, 185.

37. Ford, *Time to Heal*, 312; Marcy Bachmann, "A Cell of One's Own," *San Francisco*, May 1983, 25–26.

38. Ford, *Time to Heal*, 311–12; Kennerly, *Shooter*, 190; Helen Thomas, *Thanks for the Memories, Mr. President* (New York: Scribner, 2002), 105. On both assassination attempts, see Philip H. Melanson with Peter F. Stevens, *The Secret Service: The Hidden History of an Enigmatic Agency* (New York: Carroll and Graf, 2002), 99–104.

THE "FIRST MAMA" AND
THE ELECTION OF 1976

1. "Talking with Betty," *Newsweek*, December 29, 1975, 21.

2. *Daily News (New York)*, undated clipping, Gerald R. Ford Presidential Library, Ann Arbor, MI (GFL).

3. Myra MacPherson, "The Blooming of Betty Ford," *McCall's*, September 1975, 122.

4. David Hume Kennerly, *Shooter* (New York: Newsweek Books, 1979), 117; Hugh Sidey and Fred Ward, *Portrait of a President* (New York: Harper and Row, 1975), 35.

5. Gary Kinder, "Young Jack Ford," *Family Weekly*, February 9, 1975, 16; Jack Ford to Gerald Ford, August 18, 1974, Philip Buchen Files, GFL, Box 49, Jack Ford Folder; exhibit, Gerald R. Ford Museum, Grand Rapids, MI; *Washington Star*, October 6, 1975; *President Ford 1976 Fact Book*, GFL. Also at the Gerald R. Ford Library Web site, at http://128.83.78.237/library/document/factbook/firstfam.htm.

6. Betty Ford, *The Times of My Life* (New York: Harper and Row, 1978), 112–13; *President Ford 1976 Fact Book*, GFL. Also at the Gerald R. Ford Library Web site, http://128.83.78.237/library/document/factbook/firstfam.htm.

7. *New York Times*, June 2, 1975; Gerald R. Ford Library exhibit; *Evening Capital*, March 13, 1975. Buchen Files, box 49, GFL, President—Personal Family, Susan Ford folder; Ford, *Times of My Life*, 9.

8. Kennerly, *Shooter*, 116.

9. Candice Bergen, "An Intimate Look at the Fords," *Ladies Home Journal*, May 1975, 131; Anthony, *First Ladies*, 225; *New York Times*, July 10, 1975; "Betty

and Jerry Are at Home," *Time,* December 30, 1974, 9; Maria Downs, "Mostly Wine and Roses," unpublished manuscript, Maria Downs Papers, GFL, 27; Copy of Script for *Mary Tyler Moore Show* on display at Gerald R. Ford Museum, Grand Rapids, Michigan; Sheila Raab Weidenfeld, *First Lady's Lady: With the Fords at the White House* (New York: Putnam, 1979), 206–7; Weidenfeld to Buchen, October 18, 1975, Kenneth A. Lazarus Files, GFL, box 47, PP 5-1, First Lady folder; *Washington Post,* September 25, 1976; *Newsweek* Magazine Copy, Center for American History, University of Texas, Austin; Sidey and Ward, *Portrait,* 156–57.

10. Maria Downs, interview with author, April 16, 2004; Myra G. Gutin and Leesa E. Tobin, "'You've Come a Long Way, Mr. President': Betty Ford as First Lady," in Bernard J. Firestone and Alexej Ugrinsky, eds., *Gerald R. Ford and the Politics of Post-Watergate America,* vol. 2 (Westport, CT: Greenwood Press, 1993), 627; *Women's Wear Daily,* October 29, 1975; *Daily News (New York),* October 29, 1975; *Washington Star,* November 2, 1975.

11. Jeffrey Feinman, *Betty Ford* (New York: Award Books, 1976), 32; Carl Sferrazza Anthony, *First Ladies: The Saga of the Presidents' Wives and Their Power,* vol. 2 (New York: William Morrow, 1991), 223, 225; Stephen M. Bauer, *At Ease in the White House: The Uninhibited Memoirs of a Presidential Social Aide* (New York: Birch Lane Press, 1991), 173; Pearl Bailey, *Between You and Me: A Heartfelt Memoir on Learning, Loving, and Living* (New York: Doubleday, 1989), 95–111, 252.

12. Maria Downs, "Mostly Wine and Roses," GFL, 3; *Washington Post,* October 4, 1975; Ford, *Times of My Life,* 178.

13. "Betty and Jerry Are at Home," 9; Downs, "Mostly Wine and Roses," GFL, 75, 85a; *Women's Wear Daily,* June 18, 1975; Anthony, *First Ladies,* 223.

14. *Washington Star,* May 16, 1975, July 18, 1976, October 9, 1975; MacPherson, "Blooming of Betty Ford," 122; Maria Downs interview with author.

15. *New York Times,* June 30, 1976.

16. Gerald R. Ford, *A Time to Heal* (New York: Harper and Row, 1979), 146, 294; Bud Vestal, *Jerry Ford Up Close: An Investigative Biography* (New York: Coward, McCann, and Geoghegan, 1974), 184; *New York Times,* May 20, 1975; *Daily News (New York),* August 6, 1975; Weidenfeld, *First Lady's Lady,* 19.

17. Calloway to Weidenfeld, September 18, 1975, President Ford Committee Campaign Records: Chairman's Office, GFL, box A2, Ford, Betty folder; Robert Teeter and Stuart Spencer to Dick Cheney ("Analysis of Early Research"), November 12, 1975, James A. Reichley Files, GFL, box 3, "Theme Speeches" folder.

18. John Robert Greene, *The Presidency of Gerald R. Ford* (Lawrence: University Press of Kansas, 1995), 162–64; undated UPI Story, Sheila Weidenfeld Files, GFL, box 57, Betty Ford Campaigning folder; *Washington Post,* February 10, 1976, February 12, 1976; *New York Times,* February 12, 1976, February 27, 1976, April 12, 1976.

19. Quern to Buchen, May 14, 1975; Buchen to Quern, June 9, 1975; Buchen Files, GFL, box 9, Defense Department—Abortion Policy folder; *Newsday,* May 11, 1975; Ford to Most Rev. Joseph L. Bernardini, September 10, 1976, Sarah C. Massengale Files, GFL, box 1, Abortion—President's Position folder.

20. "A Dozen Who Made a Difference," *Time,* January 5, 1976, 19; memorandum, Cannon and Buchen to Ford, January 9, 1976; Connor to Cannon and Buchen, January 16, 1976, Buchen Files, GFL, box 1, Abortion folder.

21. Weidenfeld, *First Lady's Lady,* 246; *Chicago Tribune,* September 14, 1976.

22. Greene, *Presidency of Ford,* 162–68.

23. Undated clipping, *Washington Post,* Jack Ford to Gerald Ford (through Phil Buchen), August 18, 1974, and Buchen to Jack Ford, October 29, 1974, Buchen Files, GFL, box 49, President—Personal: Family—Jack Ford. For an article about the contributions of the entire family, see *New York Times,* March 7, 1976.

24. Press release, February 2, 1976, Weidenfeld Files, Subject Files, GFL, box 50, East Wing Staff: Pullen, Kaye folder; Lewis L. Gould, introduction to Nancy Kegan Smith and Mary C. Ryan, eds., *Modern First Ladies: Their Documentary Legacy* (Washington, DC: National Archives and Records Administration, 1989), 12; Jane Howard, "Forward Day by Day," *New York Times Magazine,* December 4, 1974, 40. By way of comparison: Rosalyn Carter's staff numbered between 21 and 24; Nancy Reagan's, 18 to 22; Barbara Bush's, 12; and Hillary Rodham Clinton's, 15. Robert Watson, *The Presidents' Wives: Reassessing the Office of First Lady* (Boulder, CO: Lynne Rienner, 2000), 112–13.

25. *Daily News (New York),* March 3, 1976; Weidenfeld, *First Lady's Lady,* 261, 263, 271–72.

26. Weidenfeld, *First Lady's Lady,* 280; Charles A. Higgenbotham to Betty Ford, April 2, 1976, White House Social Files: Subject Files, GFL, box 24, folder 13; *Democrat and Chronicle* (Rochester), April 21, 1976.

27. Kandy Stroud, *How Jimmy Won: The Victory Campaign from Plains to the White House* (New York: William Morrow, 1977), 242; *New York Times,* March 9, 1976.

28. *Guardian,* March 1, 1976 (clip found in Weidenfeld Files, GFL, box 37).

29. *Washington Star,* June 5, 1976; president's news summaries, Weidenfeld Files, General Subject File, box 57, Betty Ford—Campaigning folder.

30. *New York Times,* June 23, 1976; Ford, *Times of My Life,* 267–69; Weidenfeld, *First Lady's Lady,* 306–8.

31. See memos on many such calls in H. James Field Jr. Papers, GFL, box 1, Ford—Betty: Telephone Calls to Republican Convention Delegates folder; *New York Times,* August 18, 1976; Elizabeth Drew, *American Journal: The Events of 1976* (New York: Random House, 1977), 406.

32. Drew, *American Journal,* 492; Greene, *Presidency of Ford,* 177–79.

33. *Fact Book for 1976 Campaign,* GFL. Also at the Gerald R. Ford Library Web site, at http://128.83.78.237/library/document/factbook/firstlad.htm.

34. The transcript of the speech can be found in *New York Times,* November 4, 1976. It can also be viewed at the History Channel Web site, at http://www.historychannel.com/cgi-bin/frameit.cgi?p=http%3A//www .history channel.com/speeches/poligovt2.html; Ron Nessen, *It Sure Looks Different from the Inside* (Chicago: Playboy Press, 1978), 319.

35. *New York Times,* November 4, 1976; Ford, *Time to Heal,* 435.

"MY NAME IS BETTY FORD . . ."

1. Transcript of interview, January 2, 1977, Ron Nessen Files, Gerald R. Ford Presidential Library, Ann Arbor, MI (GFL), presidential media interviews, box 33, dated folder; *New York Times,* January 21, 1977; Pamela Warrick, "Living Out Loud," *Los Angeles Times,* November 12, 1995, E1.

2. *New York Times,* January 25, 1977; Sherry Angel, "This Ford has a Future," *50-Plus,* September 1986, 26.

3. Angel, "This Ford Has a Future," 24. Betty Ford, "The Best Years of My Life," *McCall's,* May 1993, 92; Andrea Chambers, "Frank as Ever, Former First Lady Betty Ford Describes Her Harrowing Years of Addiction," *People,* March 9, 1987, 90; *Los Angeles Times,* January 18, 1989.

4. Gloria Steinem, "Betty Ford Today: Still Speaking Out," *Ms.,* April 1984, 94; Warrick, "Living Out Loud," E2; Karen Westerberg Reyes, "There is So Much Help Out There," *Modern Maturity,* February/March 1992, 29.

5. Betty Ford, *Betty: A Glad Awakening* (Garden City, NY: Doubleday, 1987), 6, 41.

6. Ford, "Best Years of My Life," 92; James Cannon, interview with the author, August 12, 2002; "Betty Ford: One Day at a Time," *A&E Biography* (Arts and Entertainment Television Network, 1996); Ford, *Glad Awakening,* 11–12.

7. Ford, *Glad Awakening,* 13–23.

8. Ford, *Glad Awakening*, 18, 24; Chambers, "Frank as Ever," 89.

9. Phyllis Battelle, "What Liz Taylor Has Gone Through," *Ladies' Home Journal*, May 1984, 88; Betty Ford, *The Times of My Life* (New York: Harper and Row, 1978), 284–86; Ford, *Glad Awakening*, 48, 51–55.

10. Ford, *Glad Awakening*, 124.

11. For Mion's portrait of Betty Ford, see the artist's Web site, at http://www.tinamion.com/BettyFord.htm.

12. Reyes, "There Is So Much Help Out There," 29.

13. Helen Thomas, *Thanks for the Memories, Mr. President* (New York: Scribner, 2002), 103; MacPherson, "Betty Ford at 60," 137; "Betty Ford Has the Deed to a Gorgeous Home—And a New Lease on Life," *People*, March 26, 1979, 118.

14. Myra MacPherson, "Betty Ford at 60: 'My Life is Just Beginning,'" *McCall's*, March 1979, 138. See also "Betty Ford Has the Deed," 118.

15. Ford, *Times of My Life*, 292.

16. "Betty Ford," *A&E Biography*; Ford, *Glad Awakening*, 81–87; James M. West, MD, *The Betty Ford Center Book of Answers* (New York: Pocket Books, 1997), x.

17. *Los Angeles Times*, January 18, 1989; transcript, *Good Morning America* (ABC), January 15, 2002.

18. Ford, *Glad Awakening*, 93.

19. MacPherson, "Betty Ford at 60," 137; Ford, *Glad Awakening*, 95–96.

20. See the Betty Ford Center Web site, at http://www.bettyfordcenter.org; http://www.emc.org/about/bettyford.html; see also the Web site of the Addiction Resource Guide, at http://www.addictionresourceguide.com/listings/betty.html.

21. Ford, *Glad Awakening*, 95; Warrick, "Living Out Loud," *Los Angeles Times*, November 12, 1995, E2; transcript, *Morning Edition* (National Public Radio), October 18, 2002.

22. Battelle, "What Liz Taylor Has Gone Through," 88; *Washington Post*, April 8, 1993; Barnaby Conrad, *Time Is All We Have: Four Weeks at the Betty Ford Center* (New York: Arbor House, 1986), 41–45; *Chicago Tribune*, July 11, 1993.

23. Exhibit, Gerald R. Ford Museum, Grand Rapids, MI; *Los Angeles Times*, January 18, 1989; *Washington Post*, January 19, 1989.

24. See the home page for Join Together Online (Take Action Against Substance Abuse and Gun Violence), at http://www.jointogether.org/sa/news/alerts/reader/0,1854,561887,00.html; and the Web site for the National Center on Addiction and Substance Abuse at Columbia University, at http://casacolumbia.org/newsletter1457/newsletter_show.htm?doc_id=5583.

25. Angel, "This Ford Has a Future," 25; exhibit, Gerald R. Ford Museum.

26. *Atlanta Journal and Constitution,* March 8, 1994; *Boston Globe,* March 9, 1994; transcript, *Larry King Live,* March 19, 1994.

27. Chambers, "Frank as Ever," 89–90.

28. Donald G. Mathews and Jane Sherron De Hart, *Sex, Gender, and the Politics of ERA: A State and the Nation* (New York: Oxford University Press, 1990), 116.

29. See the Feminist Majority Foundation Web site, at http://www. feminist.org/research/chronicles/fc1981.html. Script for Betty Ford's Calls to Illinois State Legislators, 1981, on exhibit in Gerald R. Ford Museum; "Chronology of the Equal Rights Amendment," at http://www.now.org/issues/economic/ cea/history.html; Berenice Carroll, "Direct Action and Constitutional Rights: The Case of the ERA," in Joan Hoff-Wilson, ed., *Rights of Passage: The Past and Future of the ERA* (Bloomington: Indiana University Press, 1986), 63–75.

30. Press release in exhibit, Gerald R. Ford Museum; *Washington Post,* April 8, 1993; *New York Times,* March 26, 1991; *Washington Post,* March 26, 1991, April 8, 1993.

31. *Washington Post,* April 8, 1993; *Washington Times,* March 26, 1991.

32. *Los Angeles Times,* January 18, 1989; Ford, "Best Years of My Life," 94–95; Warrick, "Living Out Loud," E2; Phyllis Battelle, "Betty Ford Battles Arthritis— Every Day," *50-Plus,* January 1985, 48.

33. *Washington Post,* April 8, 1993; the Web site of the Michigan Women's Hall of Fame, at http://hall.michiganwomenhalloffame.org; the Web site of the Presidential Medal of Freedom, at http://www.medaloffreedom.com/BettyFord.htm; the Web site of the U.S. Mint, at http://www.usmint.gov/mint-programs/medals/ index.cfm?flash=yes&action=medal&ID=0; Angel, "This Ford Has a Future," 24; For a complete list of the awards and honors received by Betty Ford, see the Web site of the GFL, at http://www.ford.utexas.edu/grf/bbfaward.htm. A parenthetical comment: Betty Ford's exclusion from the National Women's Hall of Fame in Seneca Falls, New York, is a mystery to this author.

34. *Desert Sun* (Palm Springs, CA), October 17 and 20, 2000. For further information, see the *Desert Sun* Web site, at http://www.thedesertsun.com/topics/ bettyfordcenter20/stories/1034815869.shtml.

LEGACY

1. Robert P. Watson, *The Presidents' Wives: Reassessing the Office of First Lady* (Boulder, CO: Lynne Rienner, 2000), 56.

2. Transcript, meeting, September 4, 1974, Patricia Lindh and Jeanne Holm Files, Gerald R. Ford Presidential Library, Ann Arbor, MI (GFL), box 1, Women

appointees, dated folder; Betty Ford, *The Times of My Life* (New York: Harper and Row, 1978), 201–2; Gerald R. Ford, *A Time to Heal* (New York: Harper and Row, 1979), 240; *New York Times,* May 7, 1975; Myra G. Gutin and Leesa E. Tobin, "'You've Come a Long Way, Mr. President': Betty Ford as First Lady," in Bernard J. Firestone and Alexej Ugrinsky, eds., *Gerald R. Ford and the Politics of Post-Watergate America,* vol. 2 (Westport, CT: Greenwood Press, 1993), 628.

3. Ford, *Times of My Life,* 201–2; Robert T. Hartmann, *Palace Politics: An Inside Account of the Ford Years* (New York: McGraw-Hill, 1980), 227; Janet M. Martin, "Women Who Govern: The President's Appointments," in Mary Anne Borelli and Janet M. Martin, eds., *The Other Elites: Women, Politics, and Power in the Executive Branch* (Boulder, CO: Lynne Rienner, 1997), 58.

4. Lynda Johnson Robb, "Smithsonian Institution and Good Housekeeping Salute America's First Ladies," *Good Housekeeping,* April 1992, 74; Gil Troy, *Mr. and Mrs. President: From the Trumans to the Clintons,* 2nd ed. (Lawrence: University Press of Kansas, 2000), 207.

5. Poll results in John Pope, "Betty Ford," in Lewis L. Gould, introduction to Nancy Kegan Smith and Mary C. Ryan, eds., *Modern First Ladies: Their Documentary Legacy* (Washington, DC: National Archives and Records Administration, 1989), 652–53; "We Rate the First Ladies," *Good Housekeeping,* July 1980, 120+.

6. Quoted in Nancy J. Skarness, *First Ladies of the White House* (Ideals Publications, 2000), 73.

7. *U.S. News and World Report,* August 20, 2001.

8. Pope, "Betty Ford," 553. For a concise look at Eleanor Roosevelt's legacy, see Betty Houchin Winfield, "Madame President: Understanding a New Kind of First Lady," *Media Studies Journal* 8 (1994), 18 (1988): 59–71.

9. *New York Times,* August 10, 1974; Hope interview, videotape, on exhibit at Gerald R. Ford Museum, Grand Rapids, MI.

10. *U.S. News and World Report,* August 20, 2001.

11. For example, in Paul S. Boyer et al., *The Enduring Vision: A History of the American People* (Boston: Houghton Mifflin, 2002), those figures who are labeled as "heroes" are: George Washington, Andrew Jackson, Ulysses S. Grant, Dwight D. Eisenhower, Douglas MacArthur, John F. Kennedy, and—in the exceptions to my observation—Al Smith and Martin Luther King Jr.

12. Quoted in Barnaby Conrad, *Time Is All We Have: Four Weeks at the Betty Ford Center* (New York: Arbor House, 1986), 45.

BIBLIOGRAPHIC ESSAY

PRIMARY MATERIAL

The papers of Betty Ford, housed at the Gerald R. Ford Library (GFL; Ann Arbor, MI), consists of some seventy-five linear feet of clearly identifiable, open documents and about four feet of scattered material elsewhere. When compared to the total amount of material at the GFL—some 10,655 linear feet of material—the amount of manuscript material available that deals with the first lady would seem microscopically small. This is only true if one limits one's search to the Betty Ford Papers *proper*, where at present, only the Events File, Trip File, and Magazine File are open for research, files that contain a vast amount of rather pro forma material that is not particularly enlightening to the researcher. However, when one peruses the files of Ford White House staffers, both East and West Wing, that are available for research in the GFL, one finds that Betty Ford is one of the best documented first ladies in modern history. From the East Wing, the richest collection is the files of Sheila Weidenfeld; from the West Wing, the strongest collection is the files of David Hoopes, the White House staffer whose job description included the closest facsimile available of a liaison with the office of the first lady. Other helpful collections include: Philip Buchen (Files), James E. Connor (Files), Richard B. Cheney (Files), Maria Downs (Files), H. James Field (Files), Gerald R. Ford Vice Presidential Papers, Robert T. Hartmann (Files and Papers), Bobbie Greene Kilberg (Files), Patricia Lindh and Jeanne Holm (Files), Elizabeth O'Neill (Files), Sarah C. Massengale (Files), Ron Nessen (Files), Ron Nessen (Papers), Susan Porter (Files), Frances Kaye Pullen (Files), A. James Reichley (Papers), White House Social Office Central Files: Subject File, and William Roberts (Papers). For a workable short assessment of Betty Ford's Papers, see Kay Rohrer, "'If There Was Anything You Forgot to Ask': The Papers of Betty Ford," in Nancy Kegan Smith and Mary C. Ryan, eds., *Modern First Ladies: Their Documentary Legacy* (Washington, DC: National Archives and Records Administration, 1989). For further information on

{ 145 }

the Ford Library, see the library's Web site, at http://www.ford
.utexas.edu/. See also Gerald R. Ford: *Public Papers of the President,
1974–1977* (Washington, DC: U.S. Government Printing Office, 1978–
80). For a brief introduction to the scope of the papers of the first ladies, see Russell Bourne, "When the First Lady Speaks Her Mind,"
American Heritage 38 (September/October 1987): 108–9.

Interesting correspondence regarding the public debate over the
passage of the Equal Rights Amendment can be found in Bruce A.
Smathers Papers, Florida Department of State (see the Web site of the
Florida Bureau of Archives and Records Management, at http://www
.floridamemory.com/FloridaHighlights/ERA/ERA.cfm). The records
of the State of Michigan also hold information relevant to the life of
Betty Ford. The Michigan State Department of Health holds William
Bloomer's certificate of death (issued July 18, 1934; State Office Number
14122351), as well as her divorce decree from William Warren (issued
December 15, 1947; State Office Number 4114726). In Michigan, marriage, divorce, and death certificates are open to the public. The largest
cache of iconographic material is in the Audio Visual department of the
Ford Library. Tina Mion's paintings of the first ladies can be viewed at
the artist's Web site, at http://www.tinamion.com/BettyFord.htm.

Betty Ford has written two volumes of memoirs. They need to be
considered in tandem in order to get a full understanding of her reminiscent history. *The Times of My Life* (New York: Harper and Row, 1978)
was written immediately after Mrs. Ford left the White House, under a
joint contract signed with her husband for his own memoirs. It is a
charming book, written with the candid style that one would expect.
The story of the cancer operation is moving, and of all the memoirs of
first ladies, this book includes the most about her children and her rela-
tionships with them. But it is clear that at many points, she simply dis-
sembles about, or completely ignores, her addictions. There is nothing
in the book, for example, about her becoming addicted to painkillers
after her pinched nerve and arthritis attack. The final chapter, on "Long
Beach," is perfunctory at best; she did not want to write it and included
it only after being convinced to do so. Indeed, she only admits here to
having substance abuse *after* leaving the White House. In the opening
pages of *Betty: A Glad Awakening* (Garden City, NY: Doubleday, 1987),
Mrs. Ford admits to "a lot of honest self-deception" in *Times of My Life*
(xiv). *Glad Awakening* is an attempt to provide that part of her story—

her addictions—that she withheld in *Times,* and, for the first time, to tell the story of her recovery. The first four chapters flesh out *Times,* and the rest tells the tale of her recovery. The style utilized in the book—using direct quotations from the people closest to her in her life—can detract from the warmth of this story of discovery and recovery. Yet it is the critical rest of the story. Mrs. Ford has also written *Healing and Hope* (New York: Putnam, 2003), a volume that highlights the stories of six alumni of the Betty Ford Center, all women, and tells the story of their addictions, recovery, and life after the center.

Gerald R. Ford's *A Time to Heal* (New York: Harper and Row, 1979) helps to establish the type of relationship that Ford and his wife had from the beginning. In his treatment of his congressional years, Ford does indeed admit to a certain amount of neglect on his part, blaming the rigor of his jobs. When he discusses his presidency, with the exception of the cancer operation, the first lady is mentioned with far less frequency. For example, her role as a lobbyist for the ERA is not mentioned, nor is any role that Mrs. Ford may have had in the decision to pardon Nixon or the 1976 election campaign. Ford touches upon—albeit briefly—his family and his wife's recovery from substance abuse in Gerald R. Ford, *Humor and the Presidency* (New York: Arbor House, 1987).

Betty Ford's press secretary wrote the most detailed memoir of her first ladyship. Sheila Raab Weidenfeld, *First Lady's Lady: With the Fords at the White House* (New York: Putnam, 1979), is one of the first in the genre of political kiss-and-tell books written by former White House staffers. Written in the form of a journal, it is an often bitter look at the fight between the East and West Wings. In places—particularly Mrs. Ford's fight for the ERA—Weidenfeld offers excellent anecdotal detail, and her view that Mrs. Ford was overexposed by the Ford campaign in the 1976 presidential primaries certainly stands up to scholarly scrutiny. For another view of Weidenfeld, see Lloyd Shearer, "Sheila Weidenfeld: The First Lady's Press Secretary," *Parade,* April 25, 1976, 2–5.

For an anti–Betty Ford account that offers a useful counterpoint to Weidenfeld's book, see Robert T. Hartmann, *Palace Politics: An Inside Account of the Ford Years* (New York: McGraw-Hill, 1980). Ron Nessen, *It Sure Looks Different from the Inside* (Chicago: Playboy Press, 1978), offers a generally impassive view of the first lady. Maxine Cheshire, *Maxine Cheshire: Reporter* (Boston: Houghton Mifflin, 1978), gives her side of the Nancy and James Howe affair.

Other memoirs and contemporary analyses that deal with Betty Ford include Pearl Bailey, *Between You and Me: A Heartfelt Memoir on Learning, Loving, and Living* (New York: Doubleday, 1989); Rosalynn Carter, *First Lady from Plains* (Boston: Houghton-Mifflin, 1984); David Hume Kennerly, *Shooter* (New York: Newsweek Books, 1979); and Helen Thomas, *Thanks for the Memories, Mr. President* (New York: Scribner, 2002).

SECONDARY MATERIAL

A general point needs to be made here. Those works written after 1978, when Betty Ford entered Long Beach to begin her recovery from substance abuse, are written in the light of that knowledge. Those written before were operating from a knowledge base that included members of the First Family—most notably the first lady herself—denying the abuses in most of the printed record. The reader must assess studies of Betty Ford in that light.

A serious, scholarly biography of Betty Ford has yet to be written. Jeffrey Feinman, *Betty Ford* (New York: Award Books, 1976), is all too informally written and is based solely on newspaper and magazine sources. Yet he includes several thoughtful, analytical comments. The most recent biography, Jeffrey Ashley, *Betty Ford: A Symbol of Strength* (New York: Nova History Publications, 2003), is also a disappointment, written with only a few secondary sources, all too few citations, and a nonscholarly style.

More useful than either biography is the installment for the television series *A&E Biography* (Arts and Entertainment Television Network, 1996), entitled "Betty Ford: One Day at a Time." This hour-long documentary is particularly good for singular interviews with Steve and Susan Ford, Bill Bloomer, and Patricia Matson. Myra G. Gutin and Leesa E. Tobin, " 'You've Come a Long Way, Mr. President': Betty Ford as First Lady," in Bernard J. Firestone and Alexej Ugrinsky, eds., *Gerald R. Ford and the Politics of Post-Watergate America,* vol. 2 (Westport, CT: Greenwood Press, 1993), offers a straight life survey, with evidence gleaned from the Betty Ford Papers. Other useful general pieces include: "Elizabeth (Anne Bloomer) Ford," *Current Biography* (New York: H. W. Wilson, September 1975), 20–22; Jane Howard, "Forward Day by Day," *New York Times Magazine,* December 4, 1974, 36+; Myra MacPherson, "The Blooming of Betty Ford," *McCall's,* September, 1975, 93+; Gloria

Steinem, "Betty Ford Today: Still Speaking Out," *Ms.*, April, 1984, 41+; and Leesa E. Tobin, "Betty Ford as First Lady: A Woman for Women," *Presidential Studies Quarterly* 20 (fall 1990): 761–67.

Carl Sferrazza Anthony, *First Ladies: The Saga of the Presidents' Wives and Their Power*, vol. 2 (New York: William Morrow, 1991), includes an affectionate portrait of Betty Ford that glamorizes her family to the point of nonrecognition and downplays Betty's substance abuse and support for women's causes. For other short biographies of Betty Ford included in collections of lives of the first ladies, see Jeffrey Ashley, "Betty Ford," in Robert P. Watson, ed., *American First Ladies* (Pasadena, CA: Salem Press, 2002), 278–96; and John Pope, "Betty Ford," in Lewis L. Gould, introduction to Nancy Kegan Smith and Mary C. Ryan, eds., *American First Ladies: Their Lives and Their Legacy* (New York: Garland, 1996). See also: "Woman of the Year," *Newsweek*, December 29, 1975, 19–23; Lynn Minton, "Betty Ford Talks About Her Mother," *McCall's*, May 1976, 74+; and Susan Skog, *Embracing Our Essence: Spiritual Conversations with Prominent Women* (Deerfield Beach, FL: Health Communications, 1995).

Several of the studies of her husband's life and presidency offer some insight into the role of Betty Ford. Jerald F. terHorst, *Gerald Ford and the Future of the Presidency* (New York: Third Press, 1974), uses interviews with Mrs. Ford and her children to construct a fawning portrait of a first lady—and a first family, for that matter—with virtually no flaws. Bud Vestal, *Jerry Ford Up Close: An Investigative Biography* (New York: Coward, McCann, and Geoghegan, 1974), although thin in other regards, includes a full chapter on the first lady. *Time Magazine* correspondent Hugh Sidey and photographer Fred Ward collaborated for *Portrait of a President* (New York: Harper and Row, 1975). Sidey's glowing praise of Ford and Ward's photos of the First Family at leisure (including the famous series of the first lady pushing her husband into the pool, discussed in Chapter 5 of this book), helped to strengthen the view of the Fords as a "normal family." James Cannon, *Time and Chance: Gerald Ford's Appointment with Destiny* (New York: Harper Collins, 1994), fleshes out the story of Ford's pre–Betty Warren relationship with model Phyllis Brown, but despite making good use of an interview with Mrs. Ford, it is thin on her role in Ford's early career. See also John Robert Greene, *The Limits of Power: The Nixon and Ford Administrations* (Bloomington: Indiana University Press, 1992); John

Robert Greene, *The Presidency of Gerald R. Ford* (Lawrence: University Press of Kansas, 1995); and John Osborne, *White House Watch: The Ford Years* (Washington, DC: New Republic Books, 1977).

In many ways, the first in the genre of literature on the political partnership between a president and his spouse was Myra MacPherson, *The Power Lovers: An Intimate Look at Politics and Marriage* (New York: Putnam, 1975). A feature writer for the *Washington Post,* MacPherson looked at many Washington couples, utilizing the compelling term "power couple." To MacPherson, Betty Ford does not qualify; she is clearly treated as the archetypal "congressional wife." Lewis L. Gould, "First Ladies," *American Scholar* 55 (autumn 1986): 528–35, wrote convincingly on how to deal with the "celebrity process" of being first lady. Myra Gutin, *The President's Partner: The First Lady in the Twentieth Century* (Westport, CT: Greenwood Press, 1989), was ground zero for the modern study of the first ladies. Well researched (including interviews and archival sources), Gutin's Betty Ford is a "Political Surrogate and Independent Advocate." Edith Mayo, "The Influence and Power of the First Ladies," *Chronicle of Higher Education,* September 15, 1993, A52, bemoans American "hostility" toward women of power. Germaine Greer followed with "Abolish Her: The Feminist Case Against First Ladies," *New Republic,* June 26, 1995, 21–27, a now-famous attack against the office of the first lady, in so much as a person's *relationship* to an officeholder should not lead to power (in an answer to Greer's viewpoint, Carl Sferrazza Anthony calls her hypothesis "unrealistic"; see *New Republic,* July 31, 1995, 6).

In 1997, Gil Troy expanded upon this theme of political partnership. His *Mr. and Mrs. President: From the Trumans to the Clintons,* 2nd ed. (Lawrence: University Press of Kansas, 2000), is now the established starting point for any study of the first ladies since World War II. Although his hypotheses on Betty Ford are highly debatable (seeing her, for example, to have "hurt her husband's presidency," 4) it is a thoughtful, well-reasoned book that is not afraid to offer provocative hypotheses. Robert P. Watson's *The Presidents' Wives: Reassessing the Office of First Lady* (Boulder, CO: Lynne Rienner, 2000), roughly follows the format of the modern books on the presidency, and he ranks the first ladies using a spinoff of the paradigm offered by James David Barber in his *Presidential Character: Predicting Performance in the White House* (New Jersey: Pearson Education, 1992). Although there are errors (Mrs. Ford did not have a college education; 176), the ranking is intriguing, and the book offers a strong bibliography. For a continuation of the same themes, virtually without change, see Watson, "Ranking the Presidential Spouses," *Social Science Journal* 36, no. 1 (1999): 117–36; and "Toward a Study of the First Lady: The State of Scholarship," *Presidential Studies Quarterly* 33 (2003): 423–41. However, each of Watson's works suffers from overstatements beyond his presented facts. See particularly "The First Lady Reconsidered: Presidential Partner and Political Institution," *Presidential Studies Quarterly* 27 (1997): 805–18, which refers to Mrs. Ford as an "associate president" (814). Also, his statements that no one had seriously studied first ladies to that point is an overstatement.

Aside from these seminal works in this growing field of study, most of the literature on the first ladies is anecdotal in nature. Paul F. Boller Jr., *Presidential Wives: An Anecdotal History,* 2nd ed. (New York: Oxford University Press, 1998), is as advertised—a list of anecdotes taken from secondary sources; as is Peter Hay, *All the Presidents' Ladies: Anecdotes of Women Behind the Men in the White House* (New York: Viking, 1988). Betty Boyd Caroli, *First Ladies* (New York: Oxford University Press, 1987), although offering a broader array of secondary sources, also falls into this category. Margaret Truman, *First Ladies* (New York: Random House, 1995), has a chatty, informal style and an inordinate number of factual errors. See also Sharon Z. Alter, "First Ladies as Activists and Leaders in the Contemporary Presidency: Betty Ford to Hillary Rodham Clinton," paper prepared for delivery at the 1998 Meeting of the Midwest Political Science Association (GFL, Uncatalogued Papers); Cheryl Heckler-Feltz, *Heart and Soul of the Nation: How the Spirituality of Our First Ladies Changed America* (New York: Doubleday, 1997); and Carole Chandler Waldrup, *Presidents' Wives: The Lives of 44 Women of Strength* (Jefferson, NC: McFarland, 1989). Less useful works include: Alice E. Anderson and Hadley V. Baxendale, *Behind Every Successful President: The Hidden Power and Influence of America's First Ladies* (New York: SPI Books, 1991); James S. Rosebush, *First Lady, Public Wife* (Lanham, MD: Madison Books, 1987); and Nancy J. Skarmeas, *First Ladies of the White House* (Nashville, TN: Ideal Publications, 2000). A useful but now dated view of the literature written on the First Ladies is Lewis L. Gould, "First Ladies and the Presidency," *Presidential Studies Quarterly* 20 (fall 1990): 677–83.

The pages of the *Grand Rapids Press* and the *Grand Rapids Herald* illustrate Betty Bloomer Warren's life in the society of her city, her career as a dancer and dance instructor, and her work as a fashion director and model at Herpolscheimer's department store. Martha Graham, *Blood Memory* (New York: Doubleday, 1991); and Marian Horosko, comp., *Martha Graham: The Evolution of her Dance Theory and Training* (Chicago: a cappella books, 1991), offer little on the future first lady's career as a dancer but provide valuable background on her mentor, as well as insight into the world of modern dance that she hoped to belong to.

Oriana Jossean Kalant, *Alcohol and Drug Problems in Women: Research Advances in Alcohol and Drug Problems*, vol. 5 (New York: Plenum Press, 1980), is a useful compilation of the relevant studies. See also Hugh Davis Graham, "The Paradox of Eleanor Roosevelt: Alcoholism's Child," *Virginia Quarterly Review* 63 (spring 1987): 223–24, for both useful definitional material as well as interesting insight into the travails of a previous first lady. On Mrs. Ford's other disease, see Phyllis Battelle, "Betty Ford Battles Arthritis—Every Day," *50-Plus*, January 1985, 47–48.

For the best view of Betty Ford's life and development while second lady, three articles written from interviews given by Betty must be read as a package. Trude B. Feldman, "The Closest Family in Washington," *McCall's*, May 1974, 94+; Jean Liebman Block, "The Betty Ford Nobody Knows," *Good Housekeeping*, May 1974, 88+; and Barbara Howar, "Spotlight on Betty Ford: A New Breed of Wife in the Nation's Capital," *Family Circle*, November 1974, 96+ (although the story was published three months after Ford became president, the interview the article is based on was taken during the vice presidency) are, in themselves, important decipiers of stages of Betty's career. In them, she discusses her views on abortion and marijuana for the first time in public, and both articles allow the more difficult parts of being a political wife to shine through. Barbara Kellerman, *All The President's Kin* (New York: New York University Press, 1981), based entirely on secondary sources, labels the Ford children as "extensions" and their mother as a "Humanizer."

On the East Wing staff, see Weidenfeld, *First Lady's Lady* (above); Jane Perlez, "First Lady's Right Hand" [Nancy Howe], *New York Post*, August 31, 1974; and Frances Spatz Leighton, "New Job at the White House: Betty Ford's Best Friend" [Nancy Howe], *Family Weekly*, March 2, 1975, 29. Susan Cannon, "Betty Ford's Impact on Breast Cancer Awareness," undergraduate essay, University of Texas, Austin, 1999, synthesizes the literature in an effective manner. See also Kathryn Casey, "We Are Survivors," *Ladies Home Journal*, September 1991, 172; and Betty Rollin, *First, You Cry* (New York: Lippincott, 1976). A scholarly study of the role of the first lady as "First Hostess"—traditionally and presently a large part of her expected obligations—has yet to be written. Stephen M. Bauer, *At Ease in the White House: The Uninhibited Memoirs of a Presidential Social Aide* (New York: Birch Lane Press, 1991), is a series of anecdotes from a low-level military aide. In writing about Betty Ford, however, he seems to be mostly concerned with listing the starlets he danced with at the Fords' parties.

A strong general study of the suffrage movement, and the events leading up to the first introduction of the Equal Rights Amendment to Congress, is Sarah Hunter Graham, *Woman Suffrage and the New Democracy* (New Haven, CT: Yale University Press, 1996). Three excellent surveys of women's history during the postwar period are Flora Davis, *Moving the Mountain: The Women's Movement in America Since 1960* (Bloomington: University of Illinois Press, 1999); Sara Evans, *Tidal Wave: How Women Changed America at Century's End* (New York: Free Press, 2003); and Susan M. Hartmann, *From Margin to Mainstream: American Women and Politics Since 1960* (Philadelphia: Temple University Press, 1989). Joan Hoff-Wilson, ed., *Rights of Passage: The Past and Future of the ERA* (Bloomington: Indiana University Press, 1986), is an excellent collection of essays that offers a strong primer to its subject. For the history of the ERA from 1923 to the 1960s, see Susan Hartmann, *The Home Front and Beyond: American Women in the 1940's* (Boston: Twayne, 1982); and Leila J. Rupp and Verta Taylor, *Survival in the Doldrums: The American Women's Rights Movement, 1945 to the 1960's* (New York: Oxford University Press, 1990). For a strong case study of the ratification process in North Carolina, see Donald G. Mathews and Jane Sherron De Hart, *Sex, Gender, and the Politics of ERA: A State and the Nation* (New York: Oxford University Press, 1990). Mary Anne Borelli and Janet M. Martin, eds., *The Other Elites: Women, Politics, and Power in the Executive Branch* (Boulder, CO: Lynne Rienner, 1997), although offering little specific material on Betty Ford, offers much material—particularly statistical studies—that helps put Gerald Ford's policies toward women into a new context.

Nancy F. Cott, *The Grounding of Modern Feminism* (New Haven, CT: Yale University Press, 1987); and Josephine Donovan, *Feminist Theory:*

The Intellectual Traditions of American Feminism (New York: Frederick Ungar, 1985), are useful surveys of the subject. Also valuable as a survey is Jo Freeman, "From Suffrage to Women's Liberation: Feminism in Twentieth Century America," in Freeman, ed., *Women: A Feminist Perspective* (Mountain View, CA: Mayfield, 1995), 509–28. Also useful as a starting place is the excellent collection of articles found at the Women's History link from the History.Net Web site (http://womenshistory .about.com/mbody.html).

On the *60 Minutes* interview, see Frank Coffey, *60 Minutes: 25 Years of Television's Finest Hour* (Los Angeles: General Publishing Group, 1993); Mary Ann Borrelli, "Competing Conceptions of the First Lady-ship: Public Responses to Betty Ford's *60 Minutes* Interview," *Presidential Studies Quarterly* 31 (September 2001): 397–414; and Eliot Fremont Smith, "Reporting (Gasp!) What Betty Ford Said," *Columbia Journalism Review* 14 (November–December 1975): 15–17, who summarizes the interview and argues unconvincingly that it had little political consequence. On the two assassination attempts against her husband, see Philip H. Melanson with Peter F. Stevens, *The Secret Service: The Hidden History of an Enigmatic Agency* (New York: Carroll and Graf, 2002). The studies on the 1976 presidential election all but ignore the role of Betty Ford, Nancy Reagan, or Rosalyn Carter. For those that do mention the roles of the political partners, see Elizabeth Drew, *American Journal: The Events of 1976* (New York: Random House, 1977); and Kandy Stroud, *How Jimmy Won: The Victory Campaign from Plains to the White House* (New York: William Morrow, 1977).

The very best piece on the Betty Ford Center is Francesca Donlan, "Five Days in the House that Betty Built," *Desert Sun* (Palm Springs, CA), October 17 and 20, 2002. Donlan was allowed unprecedented access to the center and lived for five days with the female patients of Fisher Hall. Her reporting is both thoughtful and heartrending (it can be found at the newspaper's Web site, at http://www.thedesertsun.com/ topics/bettyfordcenter20/stories/1034815869.shtml). Barnaby Conrad, *Time Is All We Have: Four Weeks at the Betty Ford Center* (New York: Arbor House, 1986), is a moving book on his time as a patient at the center. It also includes a useful appraisal of Betty's address to the new patients on their first day. James M. West, MD, *The Betty Ford Center Book of Answers* (New York: Pocket Books, 1997), offers a primer on questions most frequently asked by patients at the center. It also includes a preface by Betty Ford that offers a few fresh anecdotes about the founding of the center. See also Phyllis Battelle, "What Liz Taylor Has Gone Through," *Ladies' Home Journal,* May 1984, 88. See also Betty Ford, *Healing and Hope* (above).

The overwhelming majority of articles written about Betty's postpresidential years center on her recovery from substance abuse. Of these, the most useful are: Sherry Angel, "This Ford Has a Future," *50-Plus,* September 1986, 24–26; Andrea Chambers, "Frank as Ever, Former First Lady Betty Ford Describes Her Harrowing Years of Addiction," *People,* March 9, 1987, 89; Myra MacPherson, "Betty Ford at 60: 'My Life is Just Beginning,'" *McCall's,* March 1979, 87+; Pamela Warrick, "Living Out Loud," *Los Angeles Times,* November 12, 1995, E1–E2.

Betty Houchin Winfield, "Madame President: Understanding a New Kind of First Lady," *Media Studies Journal* 8 (1994): 59–71, is a thoughtful piece, linking the legacy of Betty Ford to Hillary Rodham Clinton. On Betty as a hero, see the double issue of *U.S. News and World Report,* August 20, 2001. Dedicated to "Twenty Living American Heroes," Betty is so honored and is listed under the category of "Truth Tellers." See also Gayle Tumin, "First Ladies Restored to Prominence," *Americana* 20, no. 1 (April 1992): 54–57.

For suggestions for further reading, see John Robert Greene, *Gerald R. Ford: A Bibliography* (Westport, CT: Greenwood Press, 1974).

INDEX

Abbreviations used:
BF   Betty Ford
GF   Gerald R. Ford

ABC (American Broadcasting Company), 109
Abortion
    and BF, 32, 43–44, 92, 93–94, 114
    and GF, 44, 93–94
ACLU, 93
Adams, Abigail, 91
Addams, Jane, 55
Admiralty House (Second Family residence), 30, 31, 35
Agnew, Spiro T., 26, 101
AIDS, 114, 115
Air Force One, 82, 86
Air One (helicopter), 35, 48
Albert, Carl, 27
Alcoholism
    and BF, 3–4, 13, 25–26, 68–69, 70, 101–116 passim
    and Robert Bloomer (brother of BF), 3
    and William Bloomer, Sr. (father of BF), 3–4, 13, 102
    and William Warren, 13, 102
Alda, Alan, 75, 113
Alia, Queen (of Jordan), 38–39
Allen, Marty, 88 (photo)
Alvin Theatre, 11
American Bicentennial Park (Jerusalem), 97
American Broadcasting Company (ABC), 109
American Cancer Society, 42
    BF speech to (Nov. 7, 1975), 52

American Civil Liberties Union (ACLU), 93
American Political Science Association, 20
Anderson Junior College, 33
Angell, Jack, 79
Annenberg, Walter, 101, 108–109
Ann-Margret, 89–90
Armstrong, Anne, 119, 120
Art Train, 33
Arthritis and BF, 24, 32–33, 103, 112, 115
Assassination attempts on GF, 81–82

Bailey, Douglas, 63, 64
Bailey, Pearl, vii, 88
Bayh, Birch, 50–51, 57, 58
Bayh, Marvella, 51
Belitt, Ben, 9
Bennington College (Vermont), 8–9, 10
Bennington School of Dance, 8–9
Bethesda Naval Hospital, 45, 47, 48
Betty: A Glad Awakening (Ford), 112–113
Betty Ford Center (Palm Springs, CA), 108–116, 121, 123
Betty Ford Center for Cancer Prevention and Screening (Grand Rapids, Mich.), 112
Bicentennial of American Independence, 90–91
Black, Shirley Temple, 50–51, 132n24
Blair House, 38

Block, Herbert ("Herblock"), 92
Blodgett Memorial Medical Center
    (Grand Rapids, Mich.), 112
Blood Memory (Graham), 7
Bloomer, Elizabeth Ann. *See* Ford,
    Elizabeth Ann Bloomer Warren
    (Betty)
Bloomer, Hortense. *See* Godwin,
    Hortense Neahr Bloomer
Bloomer, Robert, 1, 3
Bloomer, William, Jr., 1, 6, 12, 33
Bloomer, William, Sr., 2, 12, 33
    alcoholism of, 3–4, 13, 102
    death of, 3, 6
    BF on, 3
Bolshoi Ballet, 103
Bradlee, Ben, 72
Breast Cancer Resource Committee,
    121
Brown, Jerry, 81
Brown, Phyllis, 17
Brown, Zora, 121
Bryn Afom, Camp, 7
Buchanan, Patrick, 26
Buchen, Philip, 16, 17, 67, 72, 73
Buckley, James, 43–44
Buendorf, Larry, 81
Burger, Warren, 36, 36 (photo)
Bush, George H. W., 88, 110, 114, 115

Cable News Network (CNN), 112
Califano, Joseph, 111
California Polytechnic University, 85
Calloway, Howard "Bo," 92, 97
Campbell, Joseph, 9
Camp David, 87
Cancer
    and BF breast cancer, 45–49, 62, 69,
        70, 92, 99, 122
    BF as advocate for awareness of,
        49–52, 112, 120–121
Cannon, James, xiv, 21, 29, 31, 33, 104
Captain and Tennille, The, 90
Carnegie Hall, 11
Carpenter, Liz, 62

Carter, Jimmy, 31, 98, 109, 117
Carter, Rosalynn, 33, 112, 192
Cash, Johnny, 88
Catto, Mrs. Henry, 38
CB Radios, 95–96
CBS (Columbia Broadcasting
    System), 75, 76
Celler, Emmanuel, 57
Central High School (Grand Rapids,
    Mich.), 7
Cheney, Dick, 40
Cheshire, Maxine, 70–72
Choice, Not An Echo, A (Schlafly), 58,
    60
Christian Reformed Church, 1
Citizen's Band Radios, 95–96
Civil Rights Act (1964), 57
Cliburn, Van, 87
Clinton, Bill, 112, 115
Clinton, Hillary Rodham, 118
CNN (Cable News Network), 112
Collingwood, Charles, 75
Columbia Broadcasting System
    (CBS), 75, 76
Columbia University, 111
Commercial Appeal, 95
"Congressional Club," 21
Congressional Gold Medal, 115
Connally, John, 27
Conservatism in Republican Party,
    59–60, 80, 93, 113, 114, 117
Constitution, U. S., 67
    Fourteenth Amendment, 54
    Nineteenth Amendment, 54, 133n40
    Twenty-Fifth Amendment, 28
    See also Equal Rights Amendment
Cooper, Gary, 16
Cornwall Divinity School (Essex,
    Mass.), 86
Cronkite, Walter, 110
Crosby, Bing, 90
Cruise, Dr. Joseph, 104, 108, 109, 110

Daniel, Clifton, 35
Deardorff, John, 63, 64

Defense, Department of, 93
Denishawn Company, 9
Depression, Great
    and Bloomer family, 2
    Palm Springs Desert Sun, 116
Deuster, Donald, 65
Dewey, Thomas, 18
Dialectic of Sex, The (Firestone), 57
Dickenson, Tandy Meams, 71, 72
Dirksen, Everett, 20
Dobrynin, Anatoly, 71
Dole, Robert, 120
Douglas, William O., 89
Downs, Maria, xiv, 74, 88–89
Dukakis, Kitty, 80

Eastman School of Dance (Roches-
    ter), 9, 10
Ebenezer Baptist Church, 31
Eisenhower, Dwight D., 40, 55, 59,
    144n11
Eisenhower, Mamie, 42, 78
Eisenhower Medical Center. *See* Betty
    Ford Center
Elections
    of 1948, 17–18
    of 1974, 37, 45
    of 1976, 43, 60, 63, 84, 85, 91–100
    of 1980, 109–110
Elizabeth II (queen), 90
Equal Pay Act (1963), 57
Equal Rights Amendment (ERA),
    xiii, 54–65, 74, 102
    and BF, 43, 61–68, 92, 99, 113–114,
        123, 117–118
    and GF, 61, 64, 74, 80
ERA-America, 68
ERA Countdown Campaign, 113
Ervin, Samuel, 57–58
Evans, Sara, 56, 57
Executive Order 11832, 74

Family Weekly, 70
Father Knows Best, 30
FBI, 82

FCC, 71, 96
Federal Bureau of Alcohol, Tobacco,
    and Firearms, 82
Federal Bureau of Investigation
    (FBI), 82
Federal Communications Commis-
    sion (FCC), 71, 96
Feminine Mystique, The (Friedan),
    24–25
Feminism, 56–57
    and BF, 61–62
Fenwick, Millicent, 114
Firestone, Leonard, 104, 108, 109, 110
Firestone, Shulamith, 57
*First Lady's Lady: With the Fords at
    the White House* (Weidenfeld),
    107–108
Florida Citizens Against Women's
    Draft, 59
Fodor, Ernest, 89
Ford, Elizabeth Bloomer Warren
    (Betty)
    and abortion, 32, 43–44, 92, 93–94,
        114
    as advocate against substance
        abuse, 111–116
    and addiction to painkillers, 32–33,
        68–69, 101–116 passim
    as administrator, 39–40
    and alcoholism, 3–4, 13, 25–26, 68–
        69, 70, 101–116 passim
    appearance on the *Mary Tyler
        Moore Show,* 87
    arthritis of, 24, 32–33, 103, 112, 115
    and assassination attempts on GF,
        81–82
    and Betty Ford Center, 108–116
    and Bicentennial of American In-
        dependence, 90–91
    as breast cancer awareness advo-
        cate, 49–52, 112, 120–121
    breast cancer of, 45–49, 62, 69, 70,
        92, 99, 122
    childhood of, 1–6
    and Congressional Gold Medal, 115

Ford, Betty *(continued)*
    as congressional wife, 21–26
    cosmetic surgery of, 106–107
    as dancer, 6–11, 31
    divorce from William Warren of,
        13–14, 17
    and election of 1948, 17–18
    and election of 1976, 91–100
    and election of 1980, 109–110
    and Equal Rights Amendment, 43,
        61–68, 92, 99, 113–114, 123, 117–118
    family of, 29–30, 84–86
    and feminism, 61–62
    and GF's absences from home, 23
    and GF's accession to the presi-
        dency, 35–37
    and GF's inauguration as presi-
        dent, 36–37
    and GF's nomination as vice presi-
        dent, 27–29
    and Martha Graham, 6, 9–11
    heart surgery of, 115
    as hero, 122–123
    as hostess in the White House, 87–
        91
    and Nancy Howe, 33–34, 39–40, 45,
        47, 69–74
    and International Women's Year,
        74–75
    legacy of, 117–123 passim
    as lobbyist, 30, 32, 53, 62–68, 111–
        118, 120–121, 123
    marriage to GF of, 16–18
    marriage to William Warren of, 12–
        15
    memoirs of, 107, 109, 111, 112–113
    as model, 10
    nervous breakdown of, 25–26, 103
    Nixon pardon and, 45, 51
    painting of, 107
    personality of, 86–87
    photos of, xviii, 4, 7, 19, 36, 48, 64,
        77, 88, 99, 105, 119
    pinched nerve of, 24

    and presidential appointments,
        118–119
    and Presidential Medal of Free-
        dom, 115
    and press, 32–33, 42–44, 51, 52–53,
        68, 75–80
    press conference of (Sept. 4, 1974),
        42–44
    psychiatric treatment of, 25–26, 103
    public opinion of, 83–84, 92, 107,
        120–121
    recovery from substance abuse of,
        103–106
    and religion, 6
    as Second Lady, 30–35, 68
    60 Minutes interview with, xiii, 75–
        80, 85, 92, 99
    as speaker, 30, 95, 97–98, 99–100
    staff of, 39–40, 52–53, 68, 69–70, 74,
        95
Ford, Elizabeth Bloomer Warren
    (Betty), speeches of:
    American Cancer Society (Nov. 7,
        1975), 52
    at Betty Ford Center, 111
    concession speech for GF by (Nov.
        3, 1976), 99–100
    Jewish National Fund Dinner
        (June 22, 1976), 97–98
    National Association of Alcohol-
        ism Treatment Programs (1986),
        115–116
    Utah State University (June 8,
        1974), 31–32
Ford, Dorothy Gardner, 19 (photo)
Ford, Gayle Ann Brumbaugh, 47, 86,
    94, 99 (photo), 104, 105 (photo)
Ford, Gerald R., Sr., 16, 19 (photo)
Ford, Gerald R., Jr.
    and abortion, 44, 93–94
    and absences from home as con-
        gressman, 23, 25–26
    accession to the presidency of, 35–
        37

as administrator, 40–41
assassination attempts on, 81–82
background of, 16–17
and Bicentennial of American Independence, 90–91
and Congressional Gold Medal, 115
as congressman, 20–21
and election of 1948, 17–18
and election of 1976, 37, 43, 91–100
and election of 1980, 109–110
and Equal Rights Amendment, 61, 64, 74, 80
family of, 29–30, 84–86
and BF breast cancer operation, 46–49
and Betty Ford Center, 109–110
and BF interview on *60 Minutes*, 79–80
and BF's addictions, 32–33
and BF's nervous breakdown, 25–26
and BF's recovery from substance abuse, 104–106
and Nancy Howe, 73
inauguration as president as, 35–37
legacy of, 122
marriage to Betty Ford of, 18
Nixon pardon by, 44–45, 51, 53, 86–87
painting of, 107
photos of, 19, 36, 48, 99, 105, 119
and press, 53
staff of, 40–41, 42, 67–68, 74, 79
as vice president designate, 26–29
as vice president, 39
and White House entertaining, 87–91
and women appointees, 118–119
Ford, Jack, xiv, 22, 23, 43, 52, 62, 76, 85, 94–95, 99 (photo), 105 (photo), 108
Ford, Janet, 20, 42
Ford, Michael, 22, 26, 47, 48, 79, 86–87, 94, 99 (photo), 105 (photo)

Ford, Steve, 22, 29, 78, 85, 94, 99 (photo), 104, 105 (photo), 106, 108
Ford, Susan, 5, 22, 23, 25–26, 27, 33, 39, 47, 48, 50, 70, 77–79, 85, 86, 94, 96, 102, 104, 105, 105 (photo), 108
Ford, Tennessee Ernie, 89
Ford, Thomas, 26
Fourteenth Amendment (U.S. Constitution), 54
Fouty, Dr. William, 45–46, 47
Friedan, Betty, 24–25
Fromm, Eric, 9
Fromme, Lynette "Squeaky," 81

Gallup Poll, 50
Gamma Delta Tau, 2
Georgetown Club, 71
George Washington University Medical School, 46
Gerald R. Ford Museum (Grand Rapids, Mich.), 50
Ghana, 132n24
Godwin, Arthur Miegs, 12, 19 (photo)
Godwin, Hortense Neahr Bloomer, 1, 2, 3, 12, 19 (photo), 33, 122
death of, 19
and BF's dancing career, 6–8, 10, 11
personality of, 5
Goldwater, Barry, 20, 20, 60
"Good Cheers," 6
Good Housekeeping, 29–30, 32, 68, 120
Good Morning America, 109
Goodwill Industries, 42
Graham, Katherine, 89
Graham, Martha, 6, 7, 9, 10, 11, 31, 89, 122, 126n17
"Graham Technique" 9–10
Grand Rapids, Mich., 1–2
Grand Rapids Press, 2
Grant, Cary, 98
Grant, Ulysses S., 144n11
Greener, William, 53
Greenwich Village Follies, 9

Gridiron Club, 95
Griffiths, Martha, 57, 61
Gutin, Myra, 51

Haig, Alexander, 26, 40
Halleck, Charles, 20
Haller, Henry, 86
Hanks, Nancy, 41, 43
Harlow, Bryce, 26
Harrison, George, 85
Harris Poll, 83–84
Hartmann, Robert T., 27, 29, 40, 41,
    47, 48
Harvard University, 58
Hatfield, Mark, 39
Hay-Adams Hotel, 87
Hays, Wayne, 97
Healthcare Leadership Coalition, 112
Hepburn, Katherine, 75
Herpolscheimer's (Department
    Store), 7, 10, 11, 13
Hewitt, Don, 75
Highway Beautification Act (1965),
    62, 118
Hills, Carla, 118
Hirohito, Emperor (of Japan), 87, 90
Hoffman, Martin, 97
Hoffman, Milton, 42, 97
Holm, Jeanne M., 119
Holton Arms Preparatory School, 33,
    85
Hoopes, David, 53
Hope, Bob, 90, 101, 107, 110
Hope, Dolores, 110, 122
House of Representatives, U. S.
    and Equal Rights Amendment, 56,
        57
    and GF, 20–21
    Judiciary Committee, 28, 35
Housing and Urban Development,
    U.S. Department of, 118
Howard, Jane, 31
Howe, James, 33, 71–74
Howe, Lise Courtney, 33, 71, 72

Howe, Nancy
    background of, 33–34
    and BF breast cancer operation, 45,
        47
    as special assistant to BF, 33–34, 39–
        40, 69–71
    and Tongsun Park scandal, 70–74,
        76
Hower, Barbara, 32
Humphrey, Doris, 9
Hushen, John, 53
Hussein, King (of Jordan), 38, 40
Hyde, Henry, 93
Hyde Amendment (abortion, 1976),
    93

International Women's Year, 74–75
International Women's Year, National
    Women's Conference (1977), 102
Ivey, Terry, 39

Jackson, Andrew, 144n11
Jaworski, Leon, 35
Jewish National Fund, 97
Johnson, Claudia Alta Taylor (Lady
    Bird), 46, 53, 62, 75, 102, 113, 118
Johnson, Lyndon B., 20, 25, 60, 86
Jonkman, Bartel, 17–18
Junior League (Grand Rapids, Mich.),
    2
Justice, U.S. Department of, 114

Kelley, Florence, 55
Kemper Arena (Kansas City, Mo.),
    98
Kendrick, Tom, 73
Kennedy, Caroline, 85
Kennedy, Edward, 112
Kennedy, Jacqueline, 42, 75, 86
Kennedy, Joan, 91
Kennedy, John F., 20, 59, 60, 144n11
Kennedy Center for the Performing
    Arts, 43, 88
Kennerly, David, 85–86

Khrushchev, Nikita, 59
King, Alberta, 31
King, Leslie Lynch, 16
King, Martin Luther, Jr., 144n11
Kissinger, Henry, 104, 109
Kissinger, Nancy, 75, 91
Knab, Douglas, 45
Korea, South, 71

Laird, Melvin, 26, 27, 71
"Lamentation" (Graham), 9
Lammerding, Nancy. *See* Ruwe,
    Nancy Lammerding
Larry King Live, 112
Library of Congress, 21
Lincoln Memorial, 113
Long Beach Naval Hospital Alcohol
    and Drug Rehabilitation Ser-
    vice, 104, 107, 108, 113
Lukash, Dr. William, 45–46, 48, 73
Lynchburg College, 33
Lyndon B. Johnson Memorial Grove
    (Va.), 46

MacArthur, Douglas, 144n11
MacPherson, Myra, 41, 68, 108
Mailer, Norman, 29
Manchester Union Leader, 79, 92
Manson, Charles, 81
Martha Graham Dance Company, 10,
    11
Mary Tyler Moore Show, 87
Matson, Patti, 39
May 7th College of Art (Peking), 106
McCall's, 30, 32, 52
McCarthy, Joseph, 59
McClendon, Sarah, 73
McGovern, George, 21
McGrory, Mary, 49–50
Michigan Board of Health, 14
Michigan Women's History Hall of
    Fame, 115
Michigan, University of, 16, 18
Mion, Tina, xiv, 106

Moore, Sara Jane, 81–82
Mostly Wine and Roses (unpublished;
    Downs), xiv
Mott, Lucretia, 54
Mount Vernon College, 86, 102

National American Women's Suffrage
    Association (NAWSA), 54
National Arthritis Foundation, 112
National Association of Alcoholism
    Treatment Programs, 115
National Broadcasting Company
    (NBC), 49, 53, 103
National Center on Addiction and
    Substance Abuse (Columbia
    University), 111–112
National Council on the Arts, 43
National Endowment for the Arts, 41,
    43
National Heart Association, 42
National Organization of Business
    and Professional Women, 63
National Orthopedic Hospital, 24
National Women's Conference
    (1977), 102
National Women's Hall of Fame,
    143n33
National Women's Party (NWP), 54,
    55
NAWSA, 54
NBC (National Broadcasting Com-
    pany), 49, 53, 103
Nessen, Ron, 51, 53, 69, 73, 79, 80, 82,
    97, 100
Newman, Jim, 17
Newman, Peg, 16–17
"New Right." *See* Conservatism in Re-
    publican Party
Newsday, 93
Newsweek, 68, 74
New York Times Magazine, 31
New York Times, 29, 50, 67, 121
Nineteenth Amendment (U.S. Con-
    stitution), 54, 133n40

Nixon, Richard M., 20, 40, 42, 47, 59, 60, 61, 86, 89, 90, 93, 94, 119
  Ford as vice presidential choice of, 26–29
  pardon of, 44–45, 51, 53, 86–87
  and press, 53
  resignation of, 35
Nixon, Pat, 27, 35–36, 39, 62, 75
No Greater Love, 42
Northern Illinois University, 63
Nutcracker Suite, The, 103
NWP (National Women's Party), 54, 55

O'Neill, Thomas P. ("Tip"), 71
Orlando, Tony, 98
Osborne, John, 80
"Other Side of Betty Ford. Six of Diamonds, The" (Mion), 107 (photo)

Pardon of Richard Nixon, 44–45, 51, 53, 86–87
Park, Tongsun, 71–74
Paul, Dr. Alice, 54–55
Pearson, Drew, 23
People (magazine), 83, 120
Philip, Prince (of England), 90
Phyllis Schlafly Report, 58, 59
Pitcher, Molly, 91
Porter, Susan, 39
Powers Modeling Agency, John Robert, 10
Presidential Medal of Freedom, 115, 126n17
Press
  and BF, 32–33, 42–44, 51, 52–53, 68, 75–80
  and GF, 53
"Primitive Mysteries" (Graham), 11
PRO-CHOICE America, 114
Pullen, Mary Frances, 95

Rabin, Leah, 75
Radio City Music Hall, 9

Reagan, Nancy, 98
Reagan, Ronald W., 60–61, 80, 84, 88, 91, 93, 94, 98, 109–110, 113, 114, 117
Red Cross Wives, 31
Reddy, Helen, 68
"Redstocking Manifesto," 56–57
Reformed Church of America, 1
Remington, Frederic, 87
Republican National Committee, 61, 74, 95
Republican Party and conservatism, 59–60, 80, 93, 113, 114, 117
Rockefeller, Happy, 51
Rockefeller, Nelson, 43–44, 60, 93, 120
Roe v. Wade, 32, 44, 59, 93
Rollin, Betty, 49
Roosevelt, Eleanor, xiii, 32, 53, 118, 121
Roosevelt, Franklin D., 55
Royal Rubber Company, 2
Ruckelshaus, Jill, 75, 114
Rumsfeld, Donald, 40, 41, 72, 74, 79
Ruwe, Nancy Lammerding, 52, 69, 74

Sadat, Anwar, 87
Safer, Morley, 76–78, 77 (photo)
Sage, Dr. Maurice, 97–98
Schlafly, Phyllis, 58–59, 60, 66–67, 102
Schwarzlose, John, 111
Senate, U.S., 112
  and Equal Rights Amendment, 55–58
  Rules Committee, 28
  Subcommittee on Constitutional Amendments, 57
September 11, 2001 terrorist attacks, 122–123
Sequoia (presidential yacht), 25
Seventeen (magazine), 86
Shah of Iran, 89
Shawn, Ted, 9
Sidey, Hugh, 44
Siena Research Institute, 120
Sills, Beverly, 87
Sinatra, Frank, 101

Sipple, Oliver, 81
60 Minutes interview with BF, xiii, 75–80, 85, 92, 99
Smith, Al, 144n11
Smith, Helen, 39, 44, 52
Smith, Mary Louise, 114
Sokolov, Anna, 9
Speeches. *See* Ford, Elizabeth Bloomer Warren (Betty), speeches of
St. Denis, Ruth, 9
St. Francis Hotel (San Francisco), 81
staff
  of BF, 39–40, 52–53, 68, 69–70, 74, 95
  of GF, 40–41, 42, 67–68, 74, 79
Stanton, Elizabeth Cady, 54
Stanton, Peggy, 38
Stevens, John Paul, 120
Stiles, Jack, 17
Stone Lake (Mich.), 7
"STOP-ERA Movement," 58
Studio 54, 87
Susan G. Komen Award, 112

Temple, Shirley. *See* Black, Shirley Temple
terHorst, Jerald, 44, 53, 68, 91
Thistlethwaite, Richard, 46
Thomas, Helen, 43, 107
"Three Parables, The," 11
Three Stooges, xiii
Thunderbird Golf Club (Rancho Mirage, CA), 101
Time, 23, 27–28, 93–94
Times of My Life, The (Ford), 107, 108
Title VII (Civil Rights Act of 1964), 57
Topeka Capitol Journal, 86
transition team to Ford presidency, 39
Travis, Calla, 7, 11
Trenton State College, 33
Troy, Gil, 78
Truman, Harry S., 35, 55, 61
Truman, Margaret, 35

Twenty-Fifth Amendment (U.S. Constitution), 28

U.S. News and World Report, 122, 123
U.S. v. Nixon, 35
United Nations, 88
United Press International (UPI), 43
University of Kansas, 102
University of Michigan, 16, 18
University of New Hampshire, 92
USS *Monterey*, 16
Utah State University, 85
  BF speech to (June 8, 1974), 31–32

VH-1 (television network), xiii
Vietnam, 60
Vogue, 23
Von Hoffman, Nicholas, 94
Von Trapp, Maria, 78

Wallace, George C., 60
Walter Reed Hospital, 72
Walters, Barbara, 101
Warren, William, 12–15, 17, 102, 127n27
Warren Commission, 20
Washington Children's Hospital, 42
Washington Hilton Hotel, 48
Washington Hospital for Sick Children, 42, 97
Washington Post, 26, 28, 70, 72, 73, 87, 89, 92
Washington State University, 85
Washington University (Mo.), 58
Washington, George, 144n11
Washington, Martha, 91
Watergate, 51
Watson, Robert, 118
Weidenfeld, Sheila, 52–53, 62, 63, 64, 68, 69, 70, 71, 72, 74, 75, 76, 78, 79, 91, 107–108
Weidman, Charles, 9
White House Historical Association, 33
Whitefish Lake (Mich.), 2, 125n3

Whitney, Dorene, 115
Will, George, 42
William and Mary, College of, 33
Williams (T.C.) High School (Alex-
   andria, Va.), 85
Williams, William Carlos, 9
Willkie, Wendell, 55
Wilson, Harold, 87
Wilson, Woodrow, 54
Winchester, Lucy, 38, 39, 52
Winter-Berger, Robert, 28
WISH (Women in the Senate and the
   House) List, 114, 115

Women's Rights Convention (1848),
   54
Worldmark Travel Inc., 85
World War II, 12, 16, 90

Yale University, 16
Yew, Lee Kuan, 87
Young and the Restless, The, 87

Zeoli, Rev. Billy, 47

ORLAND PARK
PUBLIC LIBRARY
A Natural Connection

14921 Ravinia Avenue
Orland Park, IL 60462

708-428-5100
orlandparklibrary.org